D0437405

TILT

TILT

SHIFTING YOUR STRATEGY FROM PRODUCTS TO CUSTOMERS

NIRAJ DAWAR

Harvard Business Review Press

Boston, Massachusetts

Printed in the United States of America

10 9 8 7 6 5 4 3

The web addresses referenced in this book were live and correct at the time of the book's publication but may be subject to change.

Library of Congress Cataloging-in-Publication Data

Dawar, N. (Niraj)
Tilt : shifting your strategy from products to customers / Niraj Dawar.
pages cm
ISBN 978-1-4221-8717-3 (hardback)
1. Customer relations. 2. Consumer behavior. 3. Marketing research. 4. Strategic planning. 5. Marketing—Management. I. Title.
HF5415.5.D385 2013
658.8'02—dc23

2013023637

The paper used in this publication meets the requirements of the American National Standard for Permanence of Paper for Publications and Documents in Libraries and Archives Z39.48-1992.

Contents

Preface

Why do marketers get so little respect? The CEO wonders how marketers spend their time; the chief financial officer (CFO) wonders how they spend the company's money; the sales folks think marketers are too conceptual, too abstract, and not sufficiently focused on the immediate business; and what the production and supply-chain folks think is not fit to print. The root of the problem is that for a couple of decades now, marketing hasn't been seen to be delivering competitive advantage. Since the heyday of mass media and mass brands, marketing's strategic contribution has progressively diminished. The function has become increasingly tactical, moving the needle on share points, only to lose them within a quarter or two. Think of the reasons your company is (or is not) reliably and consistently more profitable than its rivals in the industry. How many of those reasons are marketing reasons?

And yet, there are signs of a marketing resurgence in some industries. The new giants—Google, Amazon.com, Facebook, and Apple—are all marketing companies: both their value proposition and their competitive advantage are about customer information, and their success is underpinned by formidable brands. Indeed, you could argue that having been through its hardware, software, and Internet phases, Silicon Valley, that bellwether of the next frontier, is now in its marketing phase. But the marketing renaissance is not limited to the technology industry. Its effects are far-reaching and are redefining a wide range of industries in all geographic areas. Business leaders everywhere are grappling with rapidly commoditizing products and production and increasingly important customer management activities.

This book is for C-level executives involved in setting the strategic direction of a business. It is for CEOs who think they deserve to get a more strategic contribution from marketing, for CFOs who think they can get more bang for their marketing buck, and for marketing and brand managers who would like to regain some respect in the organization by contributing to the building of its sustainable competitive advantage.

Over the past twenty years, I have had the privilege of working with management teams in organizations in a wide variety of industries, from start-ups to multinationals, in various parts of the world. Today, many of the organizations are facing a new competitive landscape, where their traditional sources of competitive advantage are being neutralized as the world becomes flatter, and where new technologies rapidly erode product and production advantages that formed their bulwark against competition for decades. This book takes managers in these organizations back to basics, asking fundamental questions such as, Why do your customers buy from you rather than from your competitors? Answers to these questions reveal new opportunities to create both value for customers and new sources of competitive advantage.

Most books are written with a lot of help from friends. This one is no exception. In the preparation of this book, I have had the unwavering support of my wife, Chantal, who is also my idea vetter, my first-draft critic, and an all-around morale booster. I thank my sons for their patience as this book was being written—we'll go back to our canoeing and cycling trips soon.

I thank my colleagues at the Ivey Business School for conversations and draft reviews, for their support and flexibility. In particular I thank Mark Vandenbosch for his insights and incisive commentary. The dean, Carol Stephenson; the associate deans Roderick White and Eric Morse; and the director of the MBA program, Fraser Johnson, kindly gave me flexibility in scheduling my teaching to allow me the time to work on this book. I am grateful to my colleagues in the marketing area group for continual support.

My editor, Jeff Kehoe at Harvard Business Review Press, has a knack for crystallizing feedback in a way that immediately makes the end product better, and the editorial team at HBR Press holds manuscripts to the highest standard. It is also a genuine pleasure working with my agent, Esmond Harmsworth, of Zachary Schuster and Harmsworth. I am grateful for his insight into the publishing world, his ability to cut through the clutter to get at what matters, and his sense of humor.

Colleagues at INSEAD (in Fontainebleau and Singapore) kindly hosted me during my sabbatical years. In particular, I thank the faculty of the marketing area group for brilliant conversations over the years. My colleagues at Vlerick (Belgium) kindly hosted me during my sabbatical when the idea for this book was germinating, and in particular, I thank Philippe Haspeslagh, Steve Muylle, Marion Debruyne, and Frank Goedertier for discussions we have had on the big picture and cognitive competitive advantage. Thanks also to Flanders District of Creativity for funding and to Livia Pijakova for research assistance on the big-picture project, which fed into chapter 4.

I am grateful to John Bradley for ongoing discussions about the history of marketing and for the joint manuscript we developed many years ago in *A Future History of Marketing*. Dr. Neil Duggal provided support and insights that strengthened the backbone of this book.

Thanks to PhD students Charan Bagga, Theodore Noseworthy, and Jodie Whelan for conversations and their helpful comments on earlier drafts. I am grateful to a group of close and supportive friends who acted as advance readers for early chapters.

Courtney Hambides and Kierra Clemens kept various versions of various drafts of this book organized, formatted, numbered, and accessible so that I could find my way around them. Thank you.

And finally, to the managers at the companies where I led workshops, conducted interviews, and participated in meetings: thank you for your openness, suggestions, and other help. This book is for you.

Introduction

Tilting Downstream

"So, what business are you in?" is a classic cocktail party question to which most of us have a quick and well-practiced answer. Over the years you, like me, have probably heard many responses to the question, but in my own experience, the most common invariably describe the product, or the production facilities: "I'm in the business of PVC window frames," "I work for a company that makes risk management software," or "We are a bank." These concise, descriptive responses reveal more than we realize about how the manager sees his or her business and about its strategy.

Fifty years ago, in his seminal *Harvard Business Review* article "Marketing Myopia," Ted Levitt demonstrated the perils of too narrow a response to the innocuous cocktail party question. Many railroad companies, he argued, were driven out of business by upstart competition from new forms of transportation (trucking on the new interstate highways, and airlines), because they failed to recognize that railroad companies were in the transportation business, not merely in the railway business. Today's organizations are no less prone to the same myopia, and Levitt's insight is as applicable today as it was then. In recent years, Eastman Kodak Company endured a long and difficult decline that culminated in bankruptcy because, despite having invented digital photography, the company failed to grasp or manage the market's shift to the new technology. Levitt would say that the company mistakenly saw itself as being in the film business rather than in the imaging business. Similarly, Xerox got mired in the prosaic business of document handling, when its access to customers and its trove of research could have taken it to dominance in the information processing business, among the fastest-growth industries of the past forty years. And file BlackBerry in the category of "lessons not learned." The company became so wedded to a product feature—the physical keyboard—and overestimated its strength among enterprise customers so much that it missed the shift to touch-screen smartphones and lost its once-impregnable lead in the consumer market, and then in the corporate market, faster than anyone could have imagined.

But even beyond Levitt's insight, there is more depth to the "What business are you in?" question than meets the eye. When I listen to the responses, I look for what they tell us about the *center of gravity of the business*. The emphasis in the response hints at which part of the business the managers see as the primary driver of value and where management attention is concentrated.

A New Question

Over the past twenty years, I have asked thousands of managers around the world the "What business are you in?" question and followed it up with another: "Why do your customers buy from you rather than from your competitors?" The responses to the first question still describe the product the company sells or the production facilities. I am always bewildered at how rarely the managers mention the customer or the benefits to the customers. To many managers, the product *is* the business, just as in Levitt's era. Firms continue to spend inordinate amounts of time, effort, and resources on their products. In fact, businesses are structured around their products. Companies have product divisions and product managers, and profitability is generally measured by product (not by customer). Planning meetings and budgets are product-based, incentives and bonuses are tied to product volume moved, and the managers' hopes and aspirations are pinned on product innovation and the new-product pipeline. Building better products, conventional wisdom in these companies holds, is their pathway to a better, less price-competitive future. And why shouldn't the product define the business? After all, the product is what the business makes. Money comes in when product leaves the door, and product units are easily measured: revenue, costs, and margins can be assigned to a product unit and are correlated with the number of units made and sold.

My follow-up question aims to uncover what managers see as their particular competitive advantage, not just how they see their business—and it does one other thing: it reveals a puzzling gap between their product obsession and their customers' behavior. So why do they think their customers buy from them rather than from their competitors? The responses consist of reasons such as "They trust us," "Our reliability of supply and delivery," "Our service," "We are knowledgeable about their business," "Our experience with other such customers," "We make it seamless," "They see us as unique," "We're prominent in their consideration set," "Our reputation," and "Our brand." Rarely is a better product mentioned, and seldom is a lower price seen as the reason customers buy from the company. In other words, the answers to "Why do customers buy from us?" reside almost entirely in the *interactions* that take place in the marketplace. Trust, reliability of supply, service, knowledge, experience, and reputation cannot be made in a factory or packaged and sold off the shelf. These are *downstream* sources of value. They have their origins in specific activities, processes, and systems the firm employs to reduce the customers' risk and their costs of doing business. The wide gap between why customers buy from a company (downstream reasons) and where businesses are spending most of their effort and resources (upstream) is the reason for this book.

A Common Lexicon

Before we travel any further down this road, it's worthwhile to define some terminology. I will use the term *customer interactions* to refer to the points at which the customer comes into contact with the seller, the seller's products, or information about the seller in the marketplace. Sellers have *goals,* such as to hit $10 billion in revenue, to increase sales by 10 percent a year, to make a profit of $10 million, to be ranked number one on customer satisfaction, or to have the largest market share. Goals are more meaningful when they are defined relative to *competitors.* To achieve its goals, a firm adopts a *strategy* that spells out how the firm will create *value* for customers and outdo competitors to achieve its goals. Importantly, value need not be limited to a product. It can include services, of course, but also feelings and emotions, such as peace of mind and comfort. Firms pursue the creation of unique or differentiated value, because they know that their target segment of customers will buy more or be willing to pay more for that differentiated proposition. But firms don't just want to be able to do this once. They would like to put in place a system that reliably and consistently delivers unique or differentiated value to customers—a system that their competitors, by definition, do not have and will not have for a sustained period. In other words, firms seek *competitive advantage*: a way of creating value for customers—a way that their competitors do not possess. And the best type of competitive advantage is the kind that lasts, the kind competitors cannot match—the kind that is *sustainable.* Ideally, competitive advantage must be difficult, or even impossible, for competitors to replicate. But since no advantage lasts forever, firms invest in *innovation,* which is a way to find or make new forms of customer value that ideally lead to sustainable competitive advantage.

Your Center of Gravity

A central idea in this book is the *center of gravity* of a business. Businesses have traditionally sought competitive advantage in the *upstream*—the value-creation activities related to production and products. They succeeded by building bigger factories and taking advantage of scale; by finding new, cheaper raw materials or labor; by finding better ways to make, move, and store their inventory; and by inventing exciting products and features that competitors did not or could not replicate. The upstream seems all-important because, historically, it has been. Some of the best-run companies in history gained dominant market share and became very profitable by seizing upstream advantage:

- In the early years of the automobile industry, Ford built such a huge and streamlined factory that it drove the per-unit cost of production for the Ford Model T far below that of competitors' cars. The achievement gave Ford a significant pricing advantage in capturing market share. The soap, chemicals, food, and textiles industries were among the first to recognize the advantages of scale and assembly lines. Eventually, scale became one of the defining sources of competitive advantage in the twentieth century, reshaping every industry.
- When diamond mining and manufacturing giant De Beers pulverized its competition by gaining control of much of the world's supply of diamonds, the company enjoyed an unbeatable advantage for several decades. Few other companies in any industry have had as complete a hold on the sources of raw material as De Beers had, and even fewer used it as effectively to hammer that upstream competitive advantage into profits.
- Infosys, the fast-growing global IT services business headquartered in India, has built a formidable global advantage on the basis of its access to a seemingly inexhaustible, inexpensive, and yet flexible pool of software programmers, systems analysts, and engineers. Businesses everywhere turn to Infosys for its ability to rapidly coalesce large teams of expert software programmers to work on time-limited projects. Until recently, this advantage seemed impregnable: few other firms had that kind of access to the Indian software talent pool or the ability to inexpensively and rapidly deploy, disband, and redeploy teams of engineers according to client needs.
- Retail giant Walmart built an unbeatable network for moving inventory between its global supply chain and its stores. The scale and efficiency of the movement of goods meant that each product

unit was transported cheaply, fewer products were lost in transit, and fewer customers were lost due to stock-outs. These savings allowed the company to underprice competitors.

- The largest automobile manufacturer in the world, Toyota Motor Corporation, was once also known for its uncompromising emphasis on quality. Its quality focus pervaded every aspect of manufacturing, from the design of the cars to the layout of the assembly lines and the nurturing of quality circles on the shop floor. Through that advantage, the company built more-reliable cars that customers wanted and paid for.
- Some of the most innovative firms in the world relentlessly push the development of new products and measure the company's innovativeness in terms of the share of revenue represented by products introduced in the previous three or five years.

But the world in which these upstream giants built their success is in the midst of far-reaching change. Even the largest upstream companies find today that what they considered their unique advantage can become commonplace or irrelevant, seemingly overnight. With De Beers, this happened first after the end of the Cold War, when cheaper diamonds from the former Soviet Union began flooding the market. For Infosys, the easy days ended when other IT consulting firms such as Accenture and IBM discovered that they could replicate its army of smart, motivated Indian employees by hiring massively in India. By 2009 IBM had more employees in India than in the United States, and by 2013 the company was well on its way to neutralizing any labor cost advantage held by its Indian rivals. Walmart encountered substantially more powerful competition as third-party logistics firms and large-scale suppliers began to move goods from factory to shelf at comparable costs. With China as the production hub for so many products and multinational companies, third-party sourcing and logistics specialists such as Hong Kong–based Li & Fung turn what was once a proprietary skill into a service any competitor of Walmart can buy on the open market. Production outsourcing to contractors such as Foxconn in Asia also means that the economies and advantages of large-scale manufacturing are available to any of Foxconn's customers. You no longer have to build scale and own it to enjoy its benefits.

Companies that bask in the upstream glory of quality products are also witnessing how fleeting this advantage can be. Toyota found that its famed quality could be lost more easily than it was gained when the automaker ran squarely into a wall of negative publicity surrounding its braking systems.

The situation can also change for firms that rely on innovation. At these firms, the share of revenue accounted for by products launched in the preceding three to five years is often worn as a badge of honor. But the game changes when specialist innovation firms such as Ideo and Jump offer product innovation and design services in the open market, allowing any firm to buy the capabilities that were previously unique to innovative firms. In each of these cases, upstream advantage crumbled or eroded and leveled the playing field as competitors caught up or as unique assets, skills, and capabilities became commonly available for any competitor to buy or rent.

The proprietary access, skills, capabilities, and other assets that were at the heart of the industrial model that was dominant for 250 years are rapidly giving way to a postindustrial downstream model. In this model, value is created in the interactions with customers, competitive advantage is built and sustained in the marketplace, and the primary costs reside in acquiring, satisfying, and retaining customers.

Downstream Tilt

Three critical aspects of business have shifted downstream: the locus of competitive advantage, the locus of activities that add value (those the customer is willing to pay for), and the primary fixed costs in the business. These shifts have profound implications for strategy and the way businesses are measured, monitored, and managed. Businesses must now seek out and develop new forms of value and new sources of competitive advantage. In other words, business must try to *tilt*. They must reformulate their strategy for the downstream.

The erosion of upstream competitive advantage is not particular to one geographic location or industry. It is taking place all over the world, throughout many industries, and it affects firms of all sizes. It is driven by some powerful new forces. The most important is the increasingly rapid commoditization of products and production. Today, manufacturers just about anywhere can replicate the looks, and even the feel, of an innovative product and can bring it to market for a fraction of the price, in a fraction of the time it used to take. Even in industries whose new products are protected by patents, such as the pharmaceutical industry, competitors are undeterred and often enter the market before patent expiry by using new variants of the original molecule.

A related force is the outsourcing of the upstream activities. Even erstwhile product champions Nike and HP no longer manufacture their own products—they source from contract manufacturers, mostly in Asia. The bulk of their own effort and resources is spent in a race against time to develop tomorrow's blockbuster products, as yesterday's innovations become commonplace ever more rapidly. Outsourcing requires the standardization of tasks, processes, and quality. This standardization makes it easier to hand over production to outside suppliers, but it also makes your products and processes portable to competitors. Manufacturing, product development, and even design are becoming so undifferentiated and easily sourced that it is now increasingly difficult to build lasting advantage in these arenas. Product innovation, long thought to be the bulwark against commoditization, is itself becoming commoditized. The rapid and open flow of information and people, open markets for product design and innovation capabilities, reverse engineering, and global outsourcing have all contributed to a more Schumpeterian world in which the pace of creative destruction is accelerating.

Just look at how effortlessly new products are replicated in China. A made-in-China knockoff iPod sells for under $100; Nike shoes made in Putian, China, are practically indistinguishable from the real deal and are sold in many parts of the world as the genuine article. Legitimate emulators, too, abound in the marketplace. Many technical advances, such as wireless technology, near-field communications, and HTML5, tend to be based on industrywide standards, so that, by definition, competitors have access to them too. Many of those competitors also have access to the same third-party designers, manufacturers, and logistics experts that turn those basic technologies into products. The result is an equalization across basic product building blocks and an erosion of the advantages that used to stem from uniqueness in the upstream.

Yet the erosion of upstream advantage is not necessarily yielding to a world of fiercely competitive commodity players. In the following chapters, we will witness a shift in the center of gravity to the downstream as the locus for new sources of lasting competitive advantage. We will see how companies that grasp the importance of the downstream and tilt their center of gravity, are building businesses that will dominate the competitive landscape of the future.

In searching for lasting competitive advantage in the downstream, we are naturally faced with a dilemma. The sources of competitive advantage and examples that illustrate them are relatively new, but if we want to be sure that the competitive advantage is enduring and sustainable, we have to examine the success of the companies' strategy over a long period. To illustrate the concepts in this book, I have purposefully selected case studies that I have followed for years, and in some cases, decades, to understand the sources of their enduring success.

Costs, Value, and Competitive Advantage

All C-level managers should be able to address three questions that help them locate their business's center of gravity:

- Where is the greatest burden of your fixed costs? Is it in your factory, in your R&D, or in activities related to customer acquisition, retention, and satisfaction?
- Which of your activities do your customers most value? Which activities are they most likely to pay a premium for? Which ones

are the reasons for their loyalty? Where do these activities reside on the upstream-downstream spectrum?

- Where along the spectrum does your competitive advantage lie? What about your enduring differentiation?

The center of gravity of your business (relative to your industry peers) can determine your competitiveness. For example, in the pharmaceutical industry, despite patent protection for new molecules, the companies that have clout with physicians and patients tend to be in the driver's seat. These companies acquire the start-up with an upstream focus on product development or the established player with patent portfolios, and rarely the other way around. A firm that does not tilt downstream with its industry may find itself increasingly playing in commoditized playing fields, with shrinking margins, little say in customers' criteria of purchase, and little clout in the future course of the industry. This book is about taking control of your business's center of gravity.

Tilt Begins

Figure I-1 illustrates the increasing tilt of companies along the dimensions of cost, value, and competitive advantage. The dominant businesses of the twenty-first century are increasingly masters of the downstream. Amazon.com has ballooned into such a formidable force not because it sells better stuff, but because it sells stuff better. Its recommendation engine and peer advice provide unrivaled value to customers. Its data mining ensures that it knows, sometimes before its customers do, what they need. Its ability to connect sellers to buyers has turned it into the world's largest electronic shopping mall. Apple has struck the fear of failure into the hearts of its formerly formidable rivals, including BlackBerry, Palm, Sony, and Nokia, but not because Apple has the most comprehensively featured music player, phone, or tablet (it doesn't). Instead, Apple applies a superbly well-executed downstream strategy, including iTunes and the App Store, that matches music and

FIGURE I-1

Tilt downstream: the growing importance of downstream activities in creating value and competitive advantage

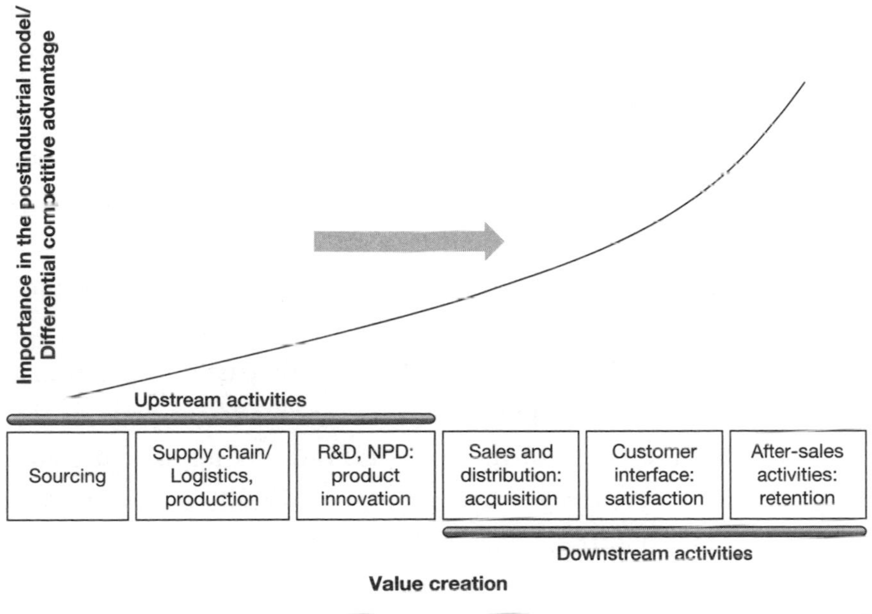

software developers with customers willing to pay a little more to get a lot more out of their gadgets.

Consider another example from the technology industry, where products have traditionally reigned supreme. At the turn of the new century, IBM recognized that more than half of corporate technology budgets were spent on installing, maintaining, and upgrading technology rather than on hardware or shrink-wrapped software. Corporate buyers were keen to ensure the reliability, compatibility, and networking of the hardware and software. Recognizing this, IBM invested heavily in delivering design and implementation services related to products that were otherwise available to its customers for free—the open-source Linux software, for example. Linux, programmed by thousands of volunteer programmers collaborating in the virtual space of the Internet, had already established a reputation as a solid and reliable enterprise-quality computing platform. Corporate customers liked that the product was free, but were slow to adopt it because they were unsure about the implementation and security risks that went with open source, or the availability of on-demand service and customization they required. Over the past decade, IBM has demonstrated that reducing those risks and customization costs for customers can be a profitable multibillion-dollar business that at the same time commoditizes the products of rivals, such as Microsoft, whose business models are designed around selling proprietary software.

In a starkly different context, but with similar conclusions, the provision of antiretroviral drugs to AIDS patients in Africa also brings out the critical value of the downstream. In the early part of this century, pharmaceutical companies pressured by activists and the press finally decided to cut the prices of their anti-HIV drugs for several countries in Africa by over 95 percent, from over $12,000 per patient per year to, in some countries, under $500. The drugs were offered to the governments of these countries for sale and distribution. But the companies soon realized there were still no takers: the pills were of little use without the downstream infrastructure of regular monitoring, testing, information delivery, and follow-up advice, little of which was available in several of those countries. In the absence of the downstream infrastructure, the product, even when almost free, was of little value.

The preceding examples are not meant to suggest that the upstream activities no longer matter, that they should be neglected, or that outsourcing them is good or bad for the company. In fact, if anything, maintaining the competitiveness of a company's upstream activities is important. Important, in that they represent table stakes—you can't play without achieving competitive parity on features, products and production, and you can't stay in the game without maintaining a certain new-product development pace. But to win, you have to achieve superiority in the downstream.

Firms that recognize that both their distinctive value creation and their competitive advantage reside in their downstream activities tend to lead the downstream tilt in their industry. But from what I have observed, even these leading firms often lack a systematic framework and processes for identifying, creating, and capturing value in the downstream. Like most players today, they have well-honed capabilities in developing new forms of value in the upstream: think of all the well-established, step-by-step processes defined by stage-gates and milestones that guide pharmaceutical firms in developing a new drug molecule, or that automobile companies use in designing a new car model. But when it comes to systematic processes for creating new forms of value in the downstream, there is often no R&D lab, no R&D manager, no R&D budget, and, most importantly, no R&D process.

Most companies continue to be run as though their center of gravity still lies upstream. Even for companies whose costs, sources of customer value, and bases of competitive advantage have tilted downstream, the business often continues to be structured, and managers continue to measure and manage, for the upstream. There is inertia, and even resistance, to moving downstream because the downstream playing field has a very different layout and a set of unfamiliar rules. *Tilt* is intended to guide businesses to a new understanding of the rules of the downstream game.

A Road Map for *Tilt*

Tilt is divided into four parts. Part 1, "Your Center of Gravity," sharpens the upstream-versus-downstream distinction and helps you locate your business on that spectrum. We will confront the gap between the upstream, where firms are allocating their current effort and remain wedded to yesterday's assets and assumptions, and the downstream, where opportunities to establish competitive advantage abound. Through some time travel, we will come to understand the roots of the industrial model that emerged in the eighteenth century and how that model defined business for over two centuries, but is rapidly becoming obsolete for the business conditions in the twenty-first. We will learn about an alternative model that places the customer rather than the factory at its core. We will see how the central strategic question of the industrial model, "How much more can we sell?" is replaced by the questions "Why do customers buy from us?" and "What else does the customer need?" These questions will lead us to the key levers in the downstream: costs and risks that customers incur in interacting with us. We will see how reducing those costs and risks is the principal downstream opportunity. We will learn why downstream activities can be a source of enduring competitive advantage and why such competitive advantage is different from upstream sources of competitive advantage. At the close of part 1, I show how businesses can reduce customers' costs and risks, by managing the flow of information in marketplace networks and by getting inside the customers' mind.

Part 2, "The Perch: Mapping Market Networks," takes a big-picture perspective on the market and shows how businesses can harness and channel information flowing through marketplace networks to reduce customers' costs and risks and create lasting competitive advantage. We will see why a perch over a network of customers, suppliers, competitors, and partners is a unique competitive asset. I will show how some businesses are mining bits of information coursing through their marketplace networks like slivers of gold, assembling large vaults of data bullion that offer fresh, new views of the market, unprecedented ways of creating value for customers, and means of building sustainable competitive advantage. We will see what makes this type of information valuable, how firms are assembling and channeling it, why it offers a basis for competitive advantage, and what makes that advantage sustainable.

In media coverage saturated with the exploits of Facebook, LinkedIn, and Twitter, it is easy to imagine that a competitive advantage based on market information is the preserve of companies in the social media space or perhaps in the broader IT industry. Certainly, companies in this space have access to new forms of very valuable data, and start-ups are being founded practically every day on the premise of new types of data and analysis techniques. Still, information-based competitive advantage is equally available to other companies and just as viable in other industries, including primary industries such as extraction (oil and gas, mining, quarrying) and manufacturing (automobiles, machine tools, pharmaceuticals), as it is in banking, software, and Internet retailing. We will examine four specific mechanisms that companies in these industries are using to harness information and to create new forms of customer value. The case studies I've chosen, including companies from a variety of industries, from quarrying to education, will illustrate this breadth of application.

Part 3, "The Deep Dive: The Competitive Playing Field Inside the Customer's Mind," will drill down to the level of the individual customers to draw implications from the dynamics of competition and the information networks inside the customers' minds. Competitive battles between brands can be long-drawn-out, costly affairs, outlasting the tenures of several management teams and often requiring outlays in the hundreds of millions, even billions, of dollars. They occur in practically every product category and in every industry, and it's not just Coke versus Pepsi: think Airbus versus Boeing, Visa versus MasterCard, Dell versus Lenovo versus Acer versus HP, Nike versus Adidas, Zantac versus Prilosec, Viagra versus Levitra versus Cialis, Colgate versus Crest, Caterpillar versus Komatsu, and so on. These battles consist of far more than just marketing tactics. They engage more than just the brand managers in these companies and consume significant resources and managerial attention. In fact, some of these competitive battles define the dynamics of their respective industries for years or even decades, pushing market segmentation and technological boundaries, driving product innovation, catalyzing mergers, and instigating corporate growth and rationalization. To the victor go the spoils of market dominance: the ability to define customer preferences, price points, terms of trade, and innovation trajectories. All of these contribute to the holy grail of business strategy: profitability and growth that exceed the industry average over sustained periods. Followers must content themselves with me-too status, living under price umbrellas created by the market leader, serving customer tastes shaped by the dominant player, and trying to live up to standards set by the alpha brand. With such long-term strategic stakes in the balance, part 3 will show that it is a mistake for any firm to enter into competition without a clear understanding of the battlefield, the company's own competitive objectives, the competitive levers, and, for good measure, a gauge of the yardsticks by which success will be defined.

Part 4, "The Bottom Line," consolidates the strategic implications of a downstream tilt. It begins with a chapter that dispels some long-standing business myths: Are better products really the way to gain competitive advantage? Are innovation and the pace of industry change dictated by technology? Can you choose your competitors? In a world of flattening playing fields, are downstream competitive advantages any more sustainable than upstream ones? That is, are the wrinkles that it offers any more exploitable and less prone to being ironed out than those in the upstream? Another chapter will introduce a new type of competitive advantage, one that is accumulative rather than prone to erosion over time. It will show how downstream advantage accrues rather than diminishes. And if you are convinced of the value of a downstream focus, you will then want to know how it changes your business. Finally, we will look at how the tilting of industries and firms affects strategy, business organization, and the marketing and sales functions. We will zoom out from specific instances and consider the downstream tilt in the context of a rapidly evolving business world, where global competition is increasingly defined by the question "Who owns the customer?"

Each of the four parts of the book consists of chapters that drive the concepts home with deep illustrative case studies taken from companies in a variety of industries and locations. The emphasis is on real-world context, and each chapter concludes with a checklist for organization and action that captures key concepts and will help you examine your own business in a new light.

TILT

Part One

Your Center of Gravity

1. Finding the New Locus of Competitive Advantage

The story of the coffee pods business that Nestlé invented and dominates serves as a wake-up call for companies in other industries facing maturing markets. For decades, Nestlé has been the world's largest coffee company. Its Nescafé brand dominates the global instant coffee market, accounting for more than 360 million of the almost 2 billion cups of coffee consumed daily on the planet.[1] But by the turn of the twentieth century, the company had identified several trends in the coffee market that were cause for concern. Eking out growth and maintaining strong margins in the maturing coffee market was becoming increasingly difficult. Despite the company's marketing and product development efforts, consumers increasingly saw instant coffee as a commodity. The broader market for roast and ground (R&G) was stagnant and intensely competitive, with several large global players, including Procter & Gamble, Kraft, Sara Lee, and strong branded ones, including Starbucks, Tchibo, Lavazza, Segafredo, and Illy, competing for share. Small price increases had been practically the only source of growth, but in a competitive marketplace, they could quickly lead to lower market share. Retailers, especially large, deep-pocketed retail groups in Europe and North America such as Ahold (the Netherlands), Sainsbury and Tesco (the United Kingdom), Carrefour (France), Walmart (the United States and Mexico), and Loblaw (Canada) were aggressively developing their private-label brands and threatening the carefully managed price-value trade-offs that had been established over decades by brands such as Nescafé. Margins began to be squeezed as packaging and distribution costs increased faster than prices. Marketing and trade expenditures, too, climbed as competition intensified. The increasingly powerful retailers demanded better margins and better terms. And in a sign that at least some parts of the market were not price-sensitive, young, trendy consumers were moving away from instant coffee altogether, to high-end gourmet R&G coffees, the only growing segment in the coffee business.

Responding to Maturing Markets

The industry's product development efforts had led to a wide variety of instant coffees from both Nestlé and its competitors. But as any brand manager will tell you, an increasing number of products clamoring for the same limited shelf space is a recipe for shifting power to the retailer. As in other grocery categories, retailers had used that power to drive down their buying prices, compete on price with other retailers, and develop and position their private-label brands, often to the disadvantage of branded-goods manufacturers such as Nestlé. Weaker brands had already been purged from the shelf and replaced with private-label stock, and now the larger players were feeling the heat to deliver on the retailers' demands to cut costs, provide high levels of service, and continuously innovate. These giant retailers in the large, affluent, developed markets had consolidated and transformed themselves from mere renters of shelf space to self-appointed custodians of the consumer relationship. Through their private-label brands and their customer loyalty programs, they were beginning to monetize the value of their proximity to consumers.

Marketing and brand-building programs such as a multipart boy-meets-girl television advertising campaign by Nestlé in the United Kingdom in the 1990s had halted the decline of its instant coffee sales in that important market, but only for a while. The campaign had bolstered sales and imbued the brand with a tinge of youth and romance, but had done little to build lasting competitive advantage. Marketing campaigns alone were an insufficient response to tectonic shifts taking place in the market. A fragmenting television landscape was making it more difficult to reach mass audiences efficiently and more expensive to build and maintain mass brands. Farther down, television itself would yield to the Internet and to on-demand programming as consumers' main sources of information. It was unclear how brands would reach mass-market consumers with the frequent reminder ads that encourage both repurchase and consumption in the coffee category.

Nestlé is hardly the only company to have experienced the maturing of a market. The signs are familiar to most managers. Competing products begin to look more and more alike, and competitors are quick to replicate every incremental product innovation and new feature. Advertising costs as well as demands from retailers and other intermediaries eat up an increasing share of the pie while brands scramble for space on crowded shelves. Category volume growth slows to a crawl as competitors start to nip at each other's consumer segments and market share in search of growth. And in the extreme, price wars break out, eroding whatever margins the companies may have had left. Future innovation is starved for lack of current cash flow, and if the players are unable to prevent it, the market can decline more quickly than anyone anticipated. With shorter product and technology life cycles, product categories are maturing more quickly than ever before, so managers don't have to stick around long to witness a market in decline: in the twenty-first century, markets mature faster than managers.

In early signs of a maturing market, companies face sustained price pushback from customers and intermediaries. The companies initially react by turning to cost-cutting measures, aiming for production and logistics efficiencies, and to product innovation if they can afford it. But escape from the perils of intense competition is not so easy—the pressures on margins are relentless. Many companies are frustrated by the rapid pace of product obsolescence and competitor emulation.

Investments in new products hardly have time to pay off before competitors nullify the differentiation or even render the products obsolete, turning the promising star products of yesterday into the dogs of today. Sony, Microsoft, and Nintendo launched their first video game consoles in the 1980s and 1990s; the companies are currently selling the eighth generation of home gaming consoles, meaning that we've already rendered seven generations obsolete. Along the way, several video game makers, including Sega and Atari, fell by the wayside, exhausted. And as each new generation hits the market, competitors are quick to match differentiating features and to whittle away at competitive leads. Nintendo's game changer, the motion-sensing Wiimotes, enjoyed a three-year lead against major competitors—an eternity in the video gaming business—but then those competitors leapfrogged the pioneer and developed much more advanced versions, leaving Nintendo in the dust. The product and feature innovation treadmill leaves even the remaining competitors panting for respite.

Far from fixing the competitive woes, innovation itself becomes a treadmill. Walk into a company in a maturing market today, and you will find its management time and dwindling resources consumed by R&D and new-product development efforts. Planning meetings and watercooler talk tend to be about next-generation products, new features, and launch calendars. Middle managers pin their hopes on the next big product introduction. But talk to the senior executives in private, and they will often tell you that despite their constant investments in innovation, bulging new-product pipelines, and the relentless drive to shrink costs and time to market, they find it impossible to shake competitors for any sustained period. And they know that their innovation efforts are not always successful, that they are playing a game of R&D roulette that may yield breakthroughs as much as it could yield breakdowns. HP, the venerable Silicon Valley tech firm long known for its cutting-edge products, withdrew the TouchPad, its promising entry into the fast-growing tablet category, after just forty-nine days on the market. It was a stunning admission of defeat in the face of relentless competition from Android and Apple tablets.

Nestlé could see the signs of the instant coffee market maturing better than any other player could. It had global reach and an integrated supply chain that extended from coffee bean agriculture to store shelves in almost every country in the world. The plateauing of sales occurred in parallel with slowing growth in the food industry in the developed markets. As the largest food company in the world, Nestlé was affected by both trends. Yet the new CEO had just promised to double the company's growth rate from 2 to 4 percent at the start of the new century. That meant that the company had to find more than $3 billion in new business *every year*, both to meet growth expectations and to compensate for businesses that were declining. Before we come back to that challenge, let's gain some insight into the roots of the industrial business model by traveling in time with a companion from eighteenth-century England.

Arkwright's Legacy

A man who started his career as a barber in Bolton in the English midlands in the 1700s became the world's first great industrialist by developing the factory system that initially turned Britain into the workshop of the world, and then the world into a workshop.[2] Richard Arkwright's impact on industry and business was at least as great as that of Henry Ford and Steve Jobs, some 150 and 250 years later, respectively. The Englishman's critical insight did not lead to the invention of a new product, but, like Ford's insights, led to new production processes. His inventiveness resided not in new product development, but, like Jobs's ingenuity, in stitching together existing innovations into something revolutionary. Arkwright realized that a slew of recent inventions for cotton spinning and weaving could be juxtaposed into an entirely new way of manufacturing: one based on the radical idea of economies of scale. By putting a large number of the machines together under one roof, he reasoned, you could achieve sourcing and production economies that were previously unheard-of. And that idea spawned a legacy that endures even today.

As the Industrial Revolution germinated in the textile industry, the replacement of human effort by water power, coupled with the mechanical efficiency of inventions like the flying shuttle and the spinning jenny, led Arkwright to understand that manufacturing costs per unit of output declined as more of these machines were gathered and operated in one place in a coordinated symphony. For thousands of years, industry had barely expanded outside the home or, at best, the village. Until Arkwright, there had been little, if any, benefit in the concentration of manufacturing: one thousand people crammed together spinning their wheels would have produced no more cotton than a thousand spinners each working away in their cottages.

But by placing into coordinated production lines a large number of specialized machines that each took on a specific task in the production of textiles, huge leaps in output could be achieved. Arkwright saw the potential and set out to realize it. Within seven years of initiating the idea of a factory, he either owned or had licensed more than 140 large-scale cotton spinning mills, dotted around Britain. With the invention of the steam engine, the constraints on the size of a factory were dramatically lifted, spurring the construction of gigantic mills. Innovations in spinning and weaving machines succeeded each other rapidly and powered factories that now enabled the production of yarn and cloth on a previously unimaginable scale. Scale had arrived—big time.

With the rapid adoption of these inventions and others that followed, yarn effectively became the first industrially manufactured product. By 1810, one spinner was as productive as two hundred had been before 1731, when John Kay invented the flying shuttle for the loom. By 1812, the cost of making cotton yarn had dropped by nine-tenths.[3] The increases in weaving capacity and the mechanization of the textile industry were rapid. The number of power looms in Great Britain mushroomed and reached 250,000 by the mid-nineteenth century. The looms were housed in some of the biggest buildings ever constructed in Europe—the factories of Dickens's England.

Mass production meant that manufacturers were in search of mass markets to absorb the now vast quantities of standardized yet inexpensive yarn and other products pouring out of the factories. Large-scale manufacturers could now do two things that smaller players could not. First, they could slash selling prices and unleash pent-up demand for cotton goods and other mass-produced products. Second, large manufacturers now had funds to invest in and develop new markets, both in nearby urban centers and in far-flung locations in Britain and its expanding and populous colonial empire. The money was used to set up wholesale and retail distribution routes to market and to persuade consumers to buy. The marketing budget had made its first appearance. Money could be invested in building markets, not just factories. Still, for at least another century or so, the capital employed in building the factories would continue to dwarf the marketing budget, and for another 250 years, the strategic imperatives of the large-scale factory would continue to drive business decisions.

Mass production rapidly ran riot through just about every industry. Entrepreneurs, businesspeople, and capitalists who seized this source of competitive advantage would quickly and decisively outperform firms with more traditional forms of competitive advantage. Those who missed it or were too slow to recognize it were either driven out of business or gobbled up by the fast-growing scale-seeking enterprises. Scale became the defining feature of success and the cornerstone of strategy. Scale-driven consolidation continues in many industries today. That is Arkwright's legacy.

The primary strategic question that drives Arkwrightian business is, "How much more of this stuff can we sell?" The amortization of the fixed costs of manufacturing, the quest for new markets, and decisions related to competitive strategy all flowed from that one question. Several important consequences of this legacy linger today in the fabric of business, despite their decreasing relevance in the twenty-first century.

The most significant consequence is that once a big factory had been built, all subsequent business decisions were taken in its shadow. The factory had shifted the cost base from one that was almost entirely variable (where percentage profit remains constant whatever the throughput) to one dominated by upstream fixed costs, where the more the producer sold, the more profitable each item became. In other words, the high fixed costs of factories had to be amortized over as large a production and sales volume as capacity would allow. This created a deeply ingrained upstream mind-set and a set of management processes and measures almost entirely predicated on consistently high-volume throughput. *How much more of this stuff can we sell?*

Narrow product ranges and volume growth became central to the production model, as they improved the profitability of existing investments. The mantra was to make the same thing over and over again. This meant that previously indispensable business tools such as rapid adaptation, customization, and nimbleness suddenly and somewhat counterintuitively became profit killers to be avoided at all costs. Marketing, too, evolved in this throughput-obsessed environment. Marketing was no use to business if it couldn't protect the engine of the system—efficient, uniform, low-cost, large-scale manufacturing. The primary role of marketing was to find mass markets for the mass-produced output pouring out of the factories.

Arkwright in the Twenty-First Century

Given the enduring importance of Arkwright's legacy, consider for a moment if he had been cryogenically frozen and then thawed to run a business in the twenty-first century. How would he respond to the challenges of today? He would probably have little problem coming to grips with most aspects of the role. He would instantly recognize that all of the key measures on his management dashboard were derived from the business model that he had invented. Capacity utilization measures would tell him how busy his factories were, and cost per unit would tell him how efficient they were. Market share would tell him how effective his production lines and sales force were, compared with those of his competitors; sales-to-asset ratios would tell him how well he was utilizing his machines and other investments. These and other management metrics would be characteristic of a familiar throughput model, with its center of gravity firmly anchored upstream and its sights set on the strategic goal of maximizing volume.

Continuing his tour of the twenty-first-century company, Arkwright would come across the innovation pipeline and R&D efforts. Here, he would congratulate management for screening innovations on the all-important question "What else can we make [given our production infrastructure]?" He would feel equally comfortable that priority was being given to "quick wins" that stood a chance of being rapidly scalable. And he would find the same mind-set codified in product- and technology-based strategies that encourage companies to identify their core competences and stick to their production and product knitting. Arkwright would also be reassured that financial hurdles based on three- or even two-year paybacks meant that the upstream capital investments were reasonably secure. In light of these indicators, he would struggle to believe that he hadn't just taken an afternoon power nap.

But as he is updated by his management team on recent developments in the manufacturing world, he might feel his pulse race at the opportunities afforded by shifting upstream fixed costs out of the system altogether. Outsourcing and flexible, efficient manufacturing have both shrunk upstream costs and turned many of them into variable costs. "Let me get this straight," he might say. "We can have all the benefits of scale, to which I am accustomed, but without having to bear any of the fixed costs? Manufacturing costs are in effect variable while still diminishing with scale?" His head spinning with the possibilities of this new business model, he would marvel at how he could have his cake and eat it too.

Still, as he sat down with the marketing and sales teams, he would see that his euphoria may have been premature: the business had not entirely dispensed with fixed costs, but had merely shifted them. The downstream costs of customer acquisition, customer satisfaction, and customer retention had ballooned as surely as the upstream costs had been shed. Sales costs were no longer just a variable per-unit commission. Much of the downstream costs were fixed. Most of the advertising, market research and analytics, brand building, customer relationship management, distribution infrastructure, data management, and after-sales service costs were incurred regardless of how many product units were sold. It would now be dawning on Arkwright that he hadn't just dozed off for a while—that there had, in fact, been a significant tilt in the structure of the business. The fixed-cost millstone of owning and operating upstream facilities was now variable, and the previously variable cost of generating sales was now both fixed and large.

How would this change his business strategy? You can hear him now: "So if the main ongoing fixed costs are advertising, promotion, listing fees, market research, and customer relationship management, and our manufacturing costs are variable, the critical resource that needs to be optimized is no longer the factory; it is the customers. We should be focusing on spreading the costs of building and maintaining the customer relationship over a variety of products that we know customers want to purchase from a trusted source. But customers are very different from factories as a locus for fixed costs. Factories are monolithic: a single entity that is good at producing one thing. Customers, on the other hand, are a collection of individuals, an aggregation of many different needs, preferences, and tastes. If our fixed costs reside in the downstream, then the question that should govern our strategy is no longer 'How much more of this stuff can we sell?' but rather 'What else do our customers need?' Our success depends not so much on economies of scale as on economies of scope."

Instead of factory throughput, our eighteenth-century manager would demand to see how many end customers he had today compared with yesterday. Instead of share of market, he would want to know his share of wallet of his existing customers. He would want to delve into deeper measures of customer engagement: how much more trusted was he than his competitors, how deeply connected to each customer? To replace cost per unit, he would obsess about costs of customer acquisition and retention, about the profitability and the lifetime value of each customer. To replace his product-line profit-and-loss statement (P&L), he might construct a customer P&L or one for each segment.

In other words, the focus of his attention and analysis would tilt from the upstream to the downstream.

But Arkwright's enthusiasm aside, businesses are not that flexible. Like a phantom limb or a deceased patriarch, the long-dismantled, shuttered, and offshored factories continue to haunt strategic discourse long after they are gone. Companies continue to be obsessed with volume (and volume measures such as market share), with the development and protection of new products (rather than markets and customers), and with the utilization of production capacity rather than the customer base. Managers continuously and misguidedly try to gain competitive advantage in the upstream playing fields that were leveled years ago.[4]

Value Shifts Downstream

Since the heyday of the Arkwright model in the twentieth century, and particularly in the last two decades, the cost bulge in many industries has tilted downstream. Production efficiencies have shrunk the share of upstream costs in the selling price of the product. The manufacturing cost of a pair of athletic shoes is usually less than 15 percent of its selling price, and the unit material and manufacturing cost of a Viagra pill is almost certainly less than 1 percent of its manufacturer-recommended retail selling price. At the same time, downstream costs have grown as a share of the selling price of the product. The cost of the armies of pharmaceutical representatives who visit doctors to convince them to prescribe pills accounts for a much greater share of the revenue pie than the manufacturing costs of the products the reps are selling. Across industries, the costs of downstream activities such as marketing, sales, and distribution now account for a significant chunk of what consumers pay for most products.

As it turns out, a large portion of the value that the customer buys also resides in downstream activities: in how the product is bought, delivered, consumed, stored, and disposed of—and more broadly, in how the customer interacts with the seller. Consider a simple example: the many ways of buying a can of Coca-Cola. A consumer can go to a supermarket or warehouse club and buy a twenty-four-pack of Coca-Cola. The pack might be priced at $5.99, so the customer ends up paying about $0.25 per can. The same customer, the next day, might find himself or herself in a park on a blazingly hot summer day. In this very different scenario, the person might gladly pay $2 for a chilled single-serve can of Coke sold at the point of thirst through a vending machine.

This customer willingly concedes a large price premium, traceable not to a better cola, but to a better way of buying and consuming the cola. Think of what the customer is paying for: he or she does not have to remember to buy the twenty-four-pack in advance, break out one can, find a place to store the rest, lug the can around, and find a way to keep it chilled all the way to the point of thirst in the park. The premium the customer is willing to pay reflects value created and captured by delivering the product for specific consumption circumstances and tailoring the offering to those circumstances. The value the consumer pays for includes *what* the consumer buys (the can of Coca-Cola), but it also includes *how* the consumer buys and consumes (the can is sold chilled, in a single serve, at the point of thirst).

VALUE = WHAT + HOW

Since the can of Coca-Cola can be purchased at the warehouse store for $0.25 or in the park for $2, the 700 percent price premium in the park reflects the value that resides in the *how*.

This incremental value is created in the downstream activities of the firm—in its interactions with the marketplace. In this instance, the 700 percent is such a significant increase that, in comparison, upstream exercises to reduce the materials, manufacturing, or inventory costs of each can of cola cannot produce anything comparable. The sort of supply-chain efficiency that made Walmart so dominant, in contrast, provides between 2 and 5 percent in cost savings. That kind of savings is, of course, extremely valuable when you are playing on an intensely competitive playing field where every penny matters and can add up to significant amounts when you have the scale of a Walmart. But the point of building a competitive advantage in the downstream is to escape that intensity of competition altogether and to think in terms other than production scale. And yes, of course, the value created in the downstream has associated costs. For Coca-Cola, these include the costs of the vending machine infrastructure, the costs of keeping the vending machine stocked, and the cans cool. But as we will see, the returns on those costs are often much larger than the returns on similar dollar costs in the upstream.

Yet in most organizations, strategic decisions are still prisoner to the imperative to spread upstream costs over ever larger product volumes. They force businesses to seek profitability in thin margins from large scale. The question "How much more of this stuff can we sell?" limits us to *what* we sell. And it neglects the substantial sources of customer value in the downstream—in the *how*. The question may be obsolete, but it still weighs on strategy and practice in many businesses in many industries today.

Percolating Downstream Value

Let's travel back to Vevey, Switzerland, in the early part of the twenty-first century to see how Nestlé lived up to its CEO's promise to deliver billions of dollars in new revenue every year by inventing a new model for coffee sales. Nestlé turned to a project that had been percolating in its skunkworks for a couple of decades. The idea and initial technology behind an "individualized" espresso coffee machine had been developed by Geneva's Batelle research institute, and Nestlé had acquired the early patents back in 1974.[5] But it took a quarter of a century to turn the intellectual property into a successful market for the Nespresso system that delivers a gourmet barista-style espresso coffee to the in-home consumer. The system consists of an espresso machine that produces a single serving of espresso at the press of a button. Since the machine uses individual aluminum capsules containing five grams of Nespresso coffee, the espresso is made without the mess and inconvenience of handling loose and wet ground coffee. But the Nespresso system is not limited to the machine. It also includes the Nespresso Club—the customers who sign up with Nespresso to order their coffee capsules online or on the phone.

The journey from the initial patents and technology to a successful market involved many incremental steps, some failures, and a lot of persistence. First, the coffee executives themselves needed to be convinced that there was a world outside of the instant coffee category that Nestlé so thoroughly dominated. There were many reasons not to adopt or champion the system: "too small a market," "not our market," and the "potential for cannibalization of our core instant coffee market," were just some of the ways of expressing inertia and remaining within the comfort zone of the perennial question "How much more instant coffee can we sell?

It took years for the potential of the new technology to sink in and for its further development to be supported inside the company. A charismatic project leader was eventually brought in from the outside to head up the development effort. And once top-level champions backed the project, the company worked to make the machines reliable, trying out the concept with the in-office segment of business customers first. The 500 percent price premium over regular coffee that was needed to cover costs was, Nestlé believed at the time, too high for the in-home consumer. The in-office segment, it was thought, would appreciate the clean, no-fuss, quality espresso of the Nespresso machines, despite the high cost. But the business segment met with mixed success. The reliability of the early machines was part of the problem.

By the turn of the century, a global consumer trend toward gourmet coffee was gathering steam. Nestlé felt the conditions were right to position the product for in-home consumers rather than just businesses. Nespresso had hit about $100 million in sales—good, but not quite in the same league as Nescafé with its billions of dollars in sales. Still, the continual refinement of the technology through the 1990s gave the company confidence that the Nespresso system could become a billion-dollar global business. But it was going to be a billion-dollar business like no other that the company had built.

The Nespresso system would have to be positioned as a super-premium in-home coffee experience. That was not easy for a company accustomed to selling mass-market products in large volumes and at low prices, through mass retailers, using mass-media advertising. The new market required a jettisoning of many core assumptions about the upstream and about volume, margins, media, distribution, and consumers. The change in focus was so great that Nestlé's decision to establish a separate company, with its own offices and housed in a separate building, to manage the Nespresso system now seemed visionary. (Nestlé Coffee Specialties, or NCS, began life in 1986.)

An early failure trying to sell Nespresso through traditional grocery retailers had fortuitously backed the company into creating its own direct distribution model for the capsules. The machines were sold through large department and specialty kitchenware stores, but the capsules could be ordered only online or on the phone, direct from the Nespresso Club. The result was slow initial uptake, but much greater control over the presentation of the product, prices, promotions, and responses to competitive reactions. Running the Nespresso Club also meant that NCS now understood the Nespresso consumer much better than it could ever have hoped for, had it sold only through traditional retail channels. Unlike Nestlé products sold through traditional retail channels, Nespresso gave Nestlé, not the retailers, the answers to the all-important marketing question "Who buys what when and at what price?"

When Nespresso finally became a worldwide hit, retailers came knocking, asking to carry the product. Nestlé declined. And when competitors began entering the fray in the late 2000s, patent wars predictably ensued. The seventeen hundred patents that Nestlé holds would help stall the challengers. But many of those patents are set to expire, and ultimately, the Nespresso Club—with its twelve million members worldwide, over three hundred direct-distribution boutiques in high-traffic upscale shopping areas of major cities, and NCS's other downstream advantages—would be the key to sustainable competitive advantage and a formidable barrier to entry for newcomers.

Nespresso has changed the coffee market forever. Individualized capsules now account for between 20 and 40 percent of the value in the $17 billion market for coffee in Europe, and the market for pod coffee is growing by 30 percent per year globally. NCS alone has sold over twenty billion of them since the year 2000, and the company had sales of over CHF 3 billion in 2010.[6] Another measure of Nespresso's downstream tilt is that 70 percent of its 8,300 employees are in direct contact with consumers.

What could Arkwright learn from Nespresso's success? If we were to distill lessons from that success as a business school case study might, we would certainly concentrate on the reasons why the in-home consumers of gourmet espresso coffee buy and consume Nespresso. This is the fundamental "Why do your customers buy from you rather than from your competitors?" question that I have asked thousands of executives over the past fifteen years. Why were customers ready, even eager, to pay five times the price of regular coffee for their shot of Nespresso? The answer for Nespresso is that customers don't mind shelling out $1 for an authentic espresso within a couple of minutes of rolling out of bed pajama-less on a Saturday morning. It sure beats the alternative of getting dressed, driving to the coffee shop, and standing in line to pay $3 for an espresso. What's more, there is little risk of stock-outs or closures due to public holidays, or of being seen in line without makeup or with an obvious hangover. If the company targets the right consumer—those who are convinced that regular R&G coffee is an inadequate substitute for espresso—the only comparison is with out-of-home coffee. The value of the coffee resides in eliminating the costs (getting dressed, going out, driving, standing in line, paying $3) and risks (stock-outs, closures, being seen out of sorts, etc.) involved with those alternatives. Nespresso delivers that value in spades and comes out looking great in comparison. And that is what makes it a $3 billion business growing organically at 20 percent per year.

How Far Do You Go?

"What is a pharmaceutical company doing in the video game business?" I asked. I was curious to understand Janssen Pharmaceutica's foray into online gaming. Was it managerial whim to ignore decades of strategy wisdom about sticking to your knitting and honing core competences, or was it a well-thought-out plan that justified the jettisoning of conventional wisdom If the latter, I wanted to understand the company's logic for the venture. Would it fit with what a downstream strategy would prescribe? Was this an extreme example of product portfolio decisions being driven by the question of what else the customer needs rather than the usual question of how much more the company could sell, or even what else the company could make with its production infrastructure.

"We're in this business because we purposefully asked, 'What else does the patient need?'" said Annik Willems, the leader of the Serious Gaming Initiative at Janssen Pharmaceutica. It was one of the first things she told me.

The pharmaceutical industry has every reason to be upstream-focused. R&D absorbs large amounts of money, blockbuster drugs have come from R&D efforts in the recent past, big R&D budgets keep competitors at bay, and successful R&D is the source of the better products that allow a company a legislated market monopoly for a defined period, in the form of patents. During the patent life of a drug, the company's strategic imperative is to push as much volume out the door as possible, so that R&D costs can be recouped and margins can fund the development of new molecules. This business model propelled pharmaceutical companies to develop some revolutionary drugs in the second half of the twentieth century. But in the early part of the twenty-first century, the model ran into headwinds. Drug prices hit ceilings in many countries as governments and insurance companies balked at the costs of new medicines. Additionally, the vagaries of R&D pipelines meant that pharmaceutical companies had to rely on mergers and acquisitions when in-house R&D came up short. And finally, competitors looking for ways around patents became litigious, driving up the costs and efforts of patent defense. Over the past decade, many pharmaceutical companies have been looking for ways to reduce their business model's dependence on continuously better products. Some are turning to the downstream.

Janssen, a pharmaceutical company with its origins and a continuing strong base in Belgium, was founded by a physician in 1953 with the goal of making better products for the treatment of the innumerable diseases that afflict humanity. By 1961, it had been acquired by the American giant Johnson & Johnson and became the principal pillar of the American company's pharmaceutical division. Over the past five decades, Janssen has developed leading drugs in the treatment of Alzheimer's disease, cancer, pain, schizophrenia, attention deficit hyperactivity disorder (ADHD), and other conditions. Starting in 2007, a high-level strategic review led Janssen to examine possible futures for pharmaceuticals.[7] The world was moving toward much greater accountability of results from pharmaceutical products and companies. Governments, insurance companies, regulatory and approval authorities, hospitals, patients, and patient groups were all demanding much more than pills from the industry: they were expecting cost-effective solutions that fit consumer needs, budgets, and lifestyles and that delivered demonstrated health results over the long term. It became evident that merely developing new molecules and adopting a transactional approach to the selling of pills was fast becoming an outdated model. The company had to engage much more deeply with stakeholders in the downstream.

Janssen's strategic review led to a companywide initiative that came to be known internally as Beyond the Pill. This initiative involved reexamining all of the touch points for each of the company's "customers," (including patients, physicians, governments, insurance companies, and other stakeholders) and asking how these touch points could be improved.

One innovative initiative that emerged from the Beyond the Pill directive was the Venture & Incubation Center, headed by Tom Aelbrecht, a forty-ish manager with an easy but determined manner, who had started his career in the IT department. Long before the strategic review, Aelbrecht had spent considerable time thinking about the big trends that were affecting the pharmaceutical industry. He had developed a presentation detailing the impact of these big trends. "Maybe it was my IT background," he told me, "but the more I examined the big trends, the more it became obvious to me that information was absolutely central to the value that we were going to deliver to our customers in the new environment—just as central as the pharmaceutical products we were developing and selling." Before long, his presentation on the big trends landed him in the marketing and sales function at the European level. When the Beyond the Pill initiative was announced, Aelbrecht knew the new direction matched the big trends he had been documenting. He considered how he could contribute. He put together a proposal to create the internal Venture & Incubation Center to examine new business opportunities developed by managers and scientists at Janssen. Teams from across the company were invited to submit proposals for new business ideas for the chance of participating in an intrapreneurial boot camp that Aelbrecht organized. After the first set of proposals came in, a few teams were selected to participate in a three-month boot camp that trained the cross-functional teams of managers to develop their business ideas and promised them a shot at presenting their polished business plans to top management.

"I got lucky that first year," said Aelbrecht. "The proposals we developed were very good, and a stellar team of top managers, including the CEO, happened to be available for the day of the final presentations. The top executives were just as impressed with the quality of business ideas as the project teams were with the engagement of the top management."

The projects short-listed by top management received a small amount of seed money and some resources (although no staff at this stage). The project teams' task was to demonstrate the validity of their assumptions and the viability of their concept over the next eighteen to twenty-four months. If they were successful, they would receive further funding and some dedicated staff. "The boot camp idea has really taken off," said Aelbrecht. "Not all projects work out, of course—these are early-stage ventures, after all. But we're getting more proposals for Beyond the Pill innovation than we had thought possible, the teams are extremely enthusiastic, and the proposals we have funded are exciting and making good progress towards becoming self-sustaining businesses."

Two of the idea teams that had applied to enter the first boot camp were eventually merged to form one Beyond the Pill business. The first team had proposed setting up e-clinics—a cost-effective online way of delivering treatment information to patients. The second related to gaming in health care. Both projects were initially considered interesting, but lacking in specifics: how would they generate new business? Could they define their value proposition in more specific terms? Could they demonstrate a viable business model? Eventually, the two proposals were combined to form a more focused project to develop an online game for seven- to twelve-year-olds diagnosed with ADHD.

Medications, including pills that Janssen had developed, generally helped ADHD patients concentrate. But the inability to concentrate was only one of their symptoms. Related behavioral problems often persisted. The game was seen as a possible solution to address three behavioral symptoms commonly observed in patients diagnosed with ADHD—poor time management, lack of planning and organization, and difficult social interactions. When I spoke with Willems, she was already running a pilot study of the first version of the online game, branded *HealSeeker*, with real patients. She was overseeing a collaboration of game development with Ranj, a "serious-gaming" development shop in the Netherlands. The company had previously designed games that were used in the selection of law students and in the training and development of leaders at a consulting firm.

Willems enumerated the advantages of a game in addressing ADHD behavioral symptoms: "Patients have difficulty concentrating, but they love the game, and we're seeing that in our tests. We limit participants to forty-five minutes of play per day. And almost all of the participants choose to play the full time allowance. Once this product launches, we'd like to be able to offer it to clinics as a complement to their counseling and therapy sessions with ADHD patients. For these patients, clinic visits are time-consuming and expensive, and they often skip them. With the game, we know we have patient interest, a means of keeping them engaged in their own treatment. They log in and complete the exercises on their own time." For now, Willems was keenly following the progress of forty-two diagnosed patients split into two groups (one group with very limited access to the game, the other with up to forty-five minutes of play time per day). She was looking forward to reviewing the data on the participants' improvement in time management, planning, and social skills. "We expect the group that has logged more play time to have significantly improved scores on every behavioral dimension," she declared confidently.

"How generalizable is this game beyond ADHD patients?" I asked her. All of us could use help with some combination of time management, planning, and social skills. They could use this in schools to teach kids how to plan and do their homework.

"We're not ruling out targeting a much larger population with this game in the future," Willems said. That's a long way beyond selling pills.

The story of video game development at Janssen points to the importance of asking what else the customer needs. The moment you ask that question, you are setting yourself up to step outside the bounds of core competences. It turns out that core competences have traditionally been defined by companies in terms of their upstream activities—the ability to make stuff. This is not surprising—firms believe they have control over these activities—more control than over customers and the marketplace.

Straying from the Knitting

Observers both inside and outside Sony long characterized its core competence as the miniaturization of consumer electronics or, slightly more broadly, the development of new consumer electronics products. Sticking to that core competence will yield the occasional blockbuster, such as the Walkman or the PlayStation. But if the company asks, "What else does the customer need?" it will eventually come up with an answer that requires it to stretch its core competence—into areas distant from the core and, perhaps, to activities where the company is not so competent. When that happens, a company like Janssen Pharmaceutica reaches out to outside specialists such as Ranj.

But at Sony, the advent of the Internet appeared to suddenly move the customer out of the company's orbit. Sony was late to the game. And yet, Sony—in the driver's seat of pop culture worldwide in the 1980s, when its revenue mushroomed from $3 billion to over $25 billion—should have realized that defining and leading customer preferences was the source of its wins and that its technology was merely an enabler. But the success was misattributed to technological prowess, to the ability of company engineers to develop new products more quickly than competitors, and to a core competence that was defined solely in terms of technology. Having missed the distribution and connective power of the Internet, the company went into a long-term slump from which it has yet to recover, despite a long series of new-product launches. Profits dipped below $1 billion by 2004, with the core consumer electronics division losing money. By the end of the decade, the entire company was losing money despite having wrung out an exceptional year of profit in 2008 when it reported a positive result of $3.3 billion, mainly the result of deep cost cutting.

During this period, first Apple raced past Sony by redefining consumer behavior and preferences in music consumption. Then Samsung caught up and forged past in both sales revenue and technology. In a press interview in 2011, Howard Stringer, outgoing CEO of an embattled Sony said, "We make so much more than we used to, . . . binoculars that can record video and goggles for watching 3D video games and movies . . . Don't tell me that Sony technology isn't great."[8] Nobody would. But what the company needed to hear was that being wedded to technology is part of the problem at Sony. It was late to the MP3 party because it didn't want to let go of CDs; it was late to flat-screen TVs because it was clinging to its proprietary Trinitron technology. And the company continues to define its success as well as its future opportunities in terms of products rather than customers. In the choice between sticking close to its knitting or remaining close to the customer, Sony has suffered from choosing the former.

Tilting downstream implies straying from the knitting. It means that the company should pursue customers' needs regardless of core competences or technology. In a world where the customer is the critical resource and where you can build, buy, or outsource competences, it makes sense to diversify your offering to fit customer needs. But this begs other strategic questions. How far from the knitting should you be willing to stray? What are the limits to what you will do in pursuit of the customer? Your strategy is as much defined by what you choose not to do as by what you choose to do. So, how far will you go?

The answer, once again, lies with the customer. It should depend on what the customer expects from you, your brand, and your company. If the customer expects Janssen Pharmaceutica to offer solutions to medical conditions and symptoms, then that is the company's remit. Janssen cannot sell sandpaper, machine tools, mutual funds, or kitchen utensils unless its customers see the coherence of the extension with the brand. In defining the customer (the patient, the payer), rather than its production plants or R&D patents, as the immovable center of its strategy, Janssen accepts that the company may be involved in the delivery of products and services in which it does not have production competence. When it strays into areas where it lacks competence, the competence will be outsourced, as with its contract with Ranj to make the *Heal-Seeker* game.

Arkwright's upstream-heavy model needs to tilt downstream in the twenty-first century. Here, strategic considerations begin with an understanding of customers and customer value, not with the factory and what it can make. You get to the answer by asking what costs and risks you can reduce for your customers in their search for, purchase of, usage of, and disposal of the kind of value you produce, not how you can generate more economies of scale. Consider your product one element of a bundle of benefits the customer requires—understand its role in that bundle, then step back and see how the entire bundle creates value, reduces risks, and reduces customer costs. Rather than ask how much more of this stuff you can sell, explore what else the customer wants. And finally, keep in mind that the price customers pay is just one element of the costs and risks they incur to consume your product, and often it is a small part of the overall costs and risks. If you seek out and enumerate those costs and risks, you'll be surprised that the source of many of those costs and risks is, in fact, your company: your business policies and programs, your interactions with customers. If you find ways to cut those costs and risks or eliminate them altogether, you create value for the customer. This is downstream value.

What Does It Take to Tilt?

The music industry was comfortably numb and facing the wrong way when the digital and Internet revolutions hit. Secure in its monopoly access to signed artists and bands, it was contentedly neglecting music consumers. Each of the major record labels had a unique stable of artists who gave the label its cachet. This uniqueness also meant that while all the labels competed for the consumers' music dollar, the labels were not in direct competition with each other. They appealed to different segments of the market with different musical tastes. The record companies signed up artists, promising them access to wide distribution and exposure in the media. Their network included intermediaries that could make or break a record: the publicists, deals with television and radio stations, and distribution contracts with record stores that bought large quantities of CDs for store shelves. Consequently, the players in the music industry thought they were sitting pretty—as brokers between the music makers and music consumers, with a lock on the supply of music and no direct competitors. So pretty, in fact, that they could continue to sell canned compilations of sixteen songs (fourteen of which few listeners wanted to hear) for a standard price of $12 to $16. It was nice work if you could get it.

Consequently, the industry was unprepared for what happened when, suddenly, music files could be shared as easily as sending an e-mail and when Napster showed that downloading music was as easy as web browsing. Internet promiscuity meant that music was bought and paid for once, but could potentially be shared by hundreds, thousands, even millions. The music industry panicked. It prayed to turn back the tide. When that did not work, record labels sued to reclaim copyright in a world of global file-sharing. They sued the keepers of music download websites, Internet service providers whose customers shared music online, the developers of file-sharing software, and the freeloading downloaders. The companies even sued a single mother of two in Minnesota for $3.6 million for having shared twenty-four songs through Kazaa, a file-sharing site. But the flood of inexpensive MP3 players just wouldn't abate. The Internet would not stop growing; nor would the sharing of music files. Between 2003 and 2007, the Recording Industry Association of America launched twenty thousand lawsuits. During the same period, the number of people sharing files online tripled.[9] CDs, the physical medium over which the music industry still had some control, were becoming obsolete faster than eight-track tapes wrapped in yesterday's newspaper. And all the industry's managers and all the industry's lawyers couldn't put the business model together again.

The music industry's very public battle against the Internet, Internet users, and Internet pirates did little to plug the leak. The dam was about to rupture. But before it burst, Steve Jobs stepped in. He came from outside the music industry. Unlike the record labels, his company, Apple, was not wedded to the upstream assets the music industry had accumulated (the recording contracts with artists, the decades of music libraries). Jobs understood that the music industry had lost control over the mode of music distribution and consumption—its downstream activities—and that it would, therefore, eventually lose control over the upstream. While the industry was busy wondering how it could rearrange the deck chairs to get back in the act, Jobs understood that the industry would sink without a major overhaul of the business model. The music industry needed to rebuild itself for the digital age, but its myopia about its own business, along with its internal rivalries and entrenched interests, prevented any serious reorg. All the while, outside observers increasingly recognized that the action had shifted downstream and the music industry had missed the boat.

Apple set out to build an organized marketplace that would create downstream value for consumers of music and allow producers the incentive to continue to produce. The genius of this approach was the recognition that the value that consumers would pay for was no longer in what was sold, but rather resided in completely reengineering how consumers bought, stored, and listened to music. None of what was in the iTunes store, or even the iPod, was a revolutionary technology or product, and almost none of the content was created or owned by Apple. MP3 players existed before the iPod; Napster, Kazaa, Gnutella, and others had already demonstrated how easy it was and how willing consumers were to share music online. Moreover, Amazon.com had established best practices in the online retail space, and the music industry still owned the content. Apple's revolutionary contribution was to stitch together a downstream solution that created enough value for end users to want to pay $0.99 for each song. Searchability, recommendations, playlists, customization, ease of use, ease of storage, legality, and "my music, anywhere" are all elements of the downstream value that pertain to how consumers found, bought, and consumed music. That, and an aesthetically thrilling customer experience, is where Apple focused its innovation efforts. More than twenty-five billion songs (and other content pieces) have since been downloaded from the iTunes store, and the iTunes business today generates more revenue than Apple did as a whole in 2004.

Why didn't the music industry think of that? Because it was still wedded to the idea that value resided entirely in the upstream, in the what, and neglected to see the opportunity for creating value in the downstream, in the how.

Initiating Tilt

How do you take a business or an industry that has for 250 years been run with an upstream obsession and turn it around to face downstream? How do you make strategy, business models, and managerial mind-sets more aware of the opportunities of the downstream? How do you get your people to recognize the value that can be created downstream for customers and the new sources of competitive advantage that can be captured there? How do you urge a business to shift its resources and tilt its center of gravity?

One answer is that you let the inevitability of the big forces do the transformation: technology, competition, regulation, and economics will each force businesses to evolve to meet the needs of the new environment. Upstream ways of doing business will generate diminishing returns and eventually become obsolete. Organizations will, through necessity, begin to look elsewhere for opportunities to create value and remain competitive. Accordingly, they will have no choice but to tilt downstream. This may be true for the economy, but it is dangerous and wishful thinking at the level of an individual organization. To avoid extinction, individual firms must proactively adapt. But organizations tend to cling to old ways of doing things. The record industry did not save itself. Perhaps the record labels *could* not save themselves. They had too much riding on the old model to let go of it. The result of decades of comfortable revenue and profits was inertia.

Furthermore, if you were to rely solely on macro external forces to direct organizational change, you would get an incoherent and ad hoc response to a wide and varied set of external imperatives. Technology will pull in a different direction than will competitive needs, and different parts of the business will adapt differently and at different speeds. Nor will coherent business models coalesce from disparate and dissipated efforts or evolve on their own—they will need to be created. Evolution and reliance on the macro forces to take their natural course are both too slow and too risky in today's competitive business world; they are not substitutes for a coherent, internally developed, proactive strategy.

Seizing advantage in the downstream can require long learning curves and, often, hefty upfront investments. Neither is easy to justify without a clear and deliberate recognition of the ultimate value of the investment. To seize downstream opportunities, firms may even need to do things that do not come naturally to them. For example, music labels may need to cooperate with longtime rivals, or a pharmaceutical firm might get involved in the video game business. Firms that lead the change, create new value for their customers, and capture new sources of competitive advantage do so because they recognize early on that the playing field is changing and that first movers stand to gain advantage that can last years and even decades.

The Upstream-Downstream Checklist

In recognition of the need to tilt downstream, a business goes through a series of "aha" moments. Consider your own business, and examine it in light of the following questions:

- ✓ Where does your business stand on the upstream-downstream spectrum? Where is its center of gravity?
- ✓ Where do the major costs in the business reside? Which activities are most valued by customers and most differentiated from competitors? Where does your competitive advantage reside?
- ✓ What do you consider the critical resources in the company? Are these upstream or downstream?
- ✓ What are your key measures of success? What do they monitor, the upstream or the downstream? Are they volume- and throughput-based measures, or are they customer-based, depth-of-relationship measures (such as the share of wallet)?
- ✓ What would your company look like if it were a downstream player? How would it be different from what it is today? How would its activities, resource and effort allocation, measures of success, and strategy be different?
- ✓ If the gap between where you are today and a downstream focus for your business is significant, what would it take to close that gap? What needs to change?
- ✓ How would a downstream focus differentiate your business from its competitors?
- ✓ How will those competitors respond, and how long will it take them to respond?
- ✓ How will you stay ahead of them?

2. Slashing Your Customers' Costs and Risks

One of the most valuable exercises that companies can engage in is to uncover the costs and risks incurred by their customers. Sainsbury, the UK retailer, changed the wine category and wine consumption in its market by reducing customer costs and risks. Wine consumption in the United Kingdom has always lagged Latin Europe, especially France and Italy. The average UK consumer drinks between twenty and twenty-five liters of wine in a year, about half the quantity glugged by drinkers in the continental wine-growing countries. Many reasons account for the gap: Britain's climate is not very well suited to grape growing, wine is not as deeply ingrained in the gastronomic culture as it is on the continent, and the British have a historical preference for beer and stronger alcohols.

But research also suggests another reason, one that consumers may not readily admit: wine intimidates them. Not because of its alcohol content or taste, of course, but because the product category is complex. Choosing the right wine requires considerable background knowledge: it helps to know your wine regions and subregions, the growers, the qualities of the grapes, the *cépage,* the years that were good and those that were middling, the right geographies, which pairings go with different types of food, which wine is best as an aperitif versus dessert, and so on. Standing before a shelf in the wine section with hundreds of wines to choose from, how does the harried consumer pick the right one? How does the bewildered novice consumer choose one wine over another? What criteria are used, what heuristics are at work? Pick the wrong wine for the boss's dinner, the wedding, or a date, and it can be embarrassing—many consumers don't even risk it. And yet, it isn't that consumers don't want to drink wine.

Spotting an opportunity, Sainsbury, the second-largest retailer in the United Kingdom, set about addressing it. Over the years, company buyers set up supply contracts with wine growers and brokers in almost every major wine-growing region of the world. Their goal: to select wines that fit Sainsbury consumers' palates, wallets, and social consumption occasions. And then, Sainsbury went one step further: its buyers work with wineries to ensure that a limited but well-selected variety of wines is presented to the consumer under the Sainsbury brand name. A private-label wine is hardly an innovation, but in many countries, including places like France, it is frowned upon. But not in Britain. Sainsbury has ensured that the brand delivers information to the consumer, and the information, alongside the product, is a large part of the value the consumer buys.

Sainsbury's private-label wine is lovingly described in Sainsbury's consumer magazine and in videos on the company website. The descriptions are intended to pique consumer interest in the category by providing helpful tips for wine selection and consumption; the shelf-talkers in the wine aisle complement this information for best uses and accompanying foods. On the bottle itself, Sainsbury's wine labels are color coded to simplify the consumer's choice and decision making. Red wines that are "light and fruity" are coded red; those that are "rich and complex" are coded blue. White wines have their own colors, and the Sainsbury House blend always carries a black label. In what is a complex and confusing category for many consumers, the Sainsbury brand cuts through the clutter, dispels myths and confusion, simplifies choice, and says, "Trust me." It does this not so much by offering a remarkably superior wine or a surprisingly cheaper price, but rather by making a regular wine *easy for the consumer to choose*. And given the company's track record in retailing, and with private labels in other product categories, it turns out that many consumers do trust the brand. Wine consumption in the United Kingdom has grown every year since Sainsbury began its branding program, and Sainsbury's wine sales have grown faster than the market. During the same period, per-capita wine consumption in France and Italy has declined.

Wine is not the only category that intimidates consumers. The average consumer or business purchases products and services in thousands of product and service categories every year. Each of those categories is populated with a few to a few hundred alternatives to choose from. And each of those alternatives is a bundle of features and attributes, some of them quite esoteric or difficult to understand. Most consumers don't really know what makes one digital camera better than another (hint: it isn't megapixels), or which phone plan is best for their usage pattern, or why two brands of air conditioners are priced so differently. Most people lack the expertise to determine which computer is superior, the means to test which car is best, the time to decide which washing machine is most durable, the inclination to learn which mutual fund will give them the best return and diversification, and the patience to find out which wall paint dries fastest. And even if they have the determination to dig into one or two or ten product categories to do their own due diligence about which choice is best for them, they cannot do so for every category—there simply isn't enough time. You can only be an expert in a few product categories.

Sainsbury's private-label wine business shows that even when a company has little direct control over the product and even if the product is no different from the competitors', there is ample room to create unique customer value in the downstream. Overwhelmed with information, choices, and decisions, customers look for shortcuts. They rely on peer and expert reviews for credible advice on their choices. They rely on simple cues and heuristics to help them pick from an exhausting array of choices ("I'll pick the heavier blender because it has a more solid feel to it"; "the thud of that car door closing is the sound of quality"; and "the vitamin in my shampoo must do something—otherwise, why would they be trumpeting it in their advertisements?").

Using one of the most important shortcuts, consumers rely on *brands* as simple proxies for quality. The Sainsbury brand tells the average and novice wine consumer as much as he or she needs to know about the wine to make a confident purchase and consume it with satisfaction. What the brand really offers is reassurance that the specific wine is the right choice for the usage occasion. Consumers see value in the brand because it reduces their risk, saving them the potential embarrassment and cost of making a poor choice. And it reduces their cost of choosing: Sainsbury's selection, branding, presentation, and information simplify consumers' choice and make it easier for them to select, buy, and, importantly, rebuy. As in other product categories, the brand is a very powerful and efficient type of risk and cost reducer that sellers use when they want to reduce the risks and costs for large numbers of buyers. We will return to brands for a closer look in part 3, but for now, let's examine the idea of costs and risks incurred by the customer in the marketplace.

Downstream Innovation

Innovation, broadly defined, is a set of activities involved in creating new forms of value for customers. You innovate to stay ahead of competitors, to escape commoditization or the perils of maturing markets. Yet many businesses interpret innovation very narrowly: they take it to mean new or better products. Innovation efforts too often devolve into new-product or new-feature development efforts. New products and features attract customer attention, gain a technological lead over competitors, and capture a few points of market share, but not for long. Yet salespeople and marketing managers seeking respite from the heat of competitive battles can't help but look expectantly over their shoulders for air cover in the form of new products or features promised by R&D or the new-product development department.

But if you're trying to build lasting competitive advantage in the downstream, you'll need to define innovation much more broadly. The folks in marketing and even sales will need to take charge of innovating rather than leaving it to the geniuses in the new-product development department alone.

The starting point for any exercise to build competitive advantage in the downstream is to uncover the hidden points of pain in the interactions between you and your customers. Three questions help enumerate these points of pain: (1) What are the hidden *costs* that your customers incur in buying and using your product or service? (2) What are the hidden *risks* that your customers incur in doing business with you? (3) Why do potential customers not buy from you (in other words, what are the costs and risks that prevent potential customers from doing business with you)?

It is not unusual if both your customers and your own team are oblivious to the costs and risks that you impose on buyers, simply for doing business with you. If you're a brewer, these costs and risks can be as simple as the cost (effort, time, and resources) that the consumer incurs to chill a beer before drinking it. If you're an enterprise software developer, they may be as complex as the risks of integrating a new organization-wide software system with the existing IT infrastructure. As you answer the question, you may find that similar costs and risks are imposed on customers by your competitors. In fact, many of the costs and risks we impose on customers are industrywide practices, and because everyone imposes them, they are widely accepted and invisible. Invisible, but still costly. When was the last time you gave a second thought to how much effort your customers expend comparing your product with your competitors'? Where do they get the information? Which criteria do they use? How many other brands do they consider? How quickly do they arrive at decisions? If you can uncover the costs and risks the customer incurs in this process and find ways to eliminate or reduce them before competitors do, you will have the basis of a downstream competitive advantage.

Businesses rarely pay enough attention to the customers' costs and risks because these aspects of a transaction tend to be invisible to the seller too: they occur either before or after the transaction, when the seller is not yet, or no longer, paying attention. The sellers' attention still tends to be focused on a narrow sliver of the overall customer interaction where money changes hands. A more comprehensive view of the customer points of contact increases your chances of uncovering customer costs and risks that competitors have not spotted.

Furthermore, in many industries, customers' costs and risks are incurred downstream, in the marketplace, while the seller's field of vision is firmly anchored upstream, in making the product or making it better. Reducing downstream costs and risks releases significant and tangible value—so much value, in fact, that often the costs and risks incurred by the customer far exceed the monetary price the customer pays for the product. In the Coca-Cola example in the previous chapter, the value a customer places on a can of Coke at the right time and place, in the right single-can format, and at the right temperature exceeds the value of eight cans of cola sold in a supermarket. Yet we rarely spend time systematically uncovering these types of costs and risks; they are seldom discussed at strategy or marketing meetings and are scarcely, if ever, seen as a potential source of innovation or competitive advantage. In this chapter, we'll look at examples of companies that *have* asked what costs and risks customers incur and developed downstream innovations to eliminate them.

Invisible Costs

A few years ago, a senior executive in the automobile industry, Wolfgang Reitzle, proposed a radically new idea. At the time, Reitzle was the CEO of the Premier Auto Group (PAG), the luxury-brand division of Ford. PAG sold cars to affluent customers around the world. The automobile market has always been segmented by the buyer's income and family size, and carmakers develop different brands or models to target each segment. The Chevy segment of consumers is different from the Cadillac segment, the Mini segment is different from the BMW 7 series segment, the Corvette segment is different from the minivan segment, and so on.

With its customers generally in the higher income brackets, PAG addressed their needs with brands such as Jaguar, Land Rover, Aston

Martin, Volvo, and Lincoln. Many PAG customers live in urban environments, where owning more than one car is a hassle, mainly because of parking limitations. Furthermore, many of these customers are mobile, traveling frequently both for business and for pleasure. Reitzle realized that PAG and all of its competitors were selling a fairly rigid solution (essentially a metal box on four wheels) to customers whose needs varied from day to day. For example, one jet-set customer may need several types of vehicles: a large sedan for highway driving; a small, easily parked car for getting around in the city; a 4x4 for the skiing holiday; and a convertible for the beach. What's more, many of these cars may be required far from home, in a different city or country or on a different continent.

In other words, Reitzle realized that the rigid metal vehicles that car companies sell provide only a partial solution to the customers' car needs, part of the time. A more flexible and complete value proposition could be delivered if automobile companies would consider devising a "mobility solution," Reitzle suggested, and see themselves as mobility companies. In essence, he suggested devising a contract that allows the customer the use of an occasion-appropriate vehicle at locations of their choice around the world. Customers could pay a premium price, say, $50,000 to cover a two-year period, to have the convenience of requesting any car in the company's stable, anywhere in the world, with a twenty-four-hour notice, provided they used only one car at any given time. They could have the convertible on weekends, and the city car or the limousine on weekdays, and the 4x4 on landing in Dallas or Dubai. This was a radical proposal in an industry whose identity is closely tied to its factories and its products and where customers' identities, too, are closely projected through the cars they own and drive. More than most others, this industry views the world through the prism of its upstream infrastructure and its products.

The starting point in the development of a mobility solution is the identification of the hidden costs that the car companies impose on consumers. Segmentation pigeonholes consumers into predefined niches that automakers target with a product they believe fits the niche's needs.

Production constraints make the products rigid—a vehicle can either be a minivan or a convertible; it cannot be both. In buying a product, the customer incurs an opportunity cost: he or she commits to a seller-defined bundle and forgoes the benefits of other potential feature bundles on the market. The sedan owner gives up the dream of a convertible, the convertible owner bears the cost of not having a roomy SUV, and so on. But clearly, the same customer may belong to different segments on different occasions—it's just that our rigid products and production processes cannot cope with that kind of flexibility. So we assume away that complexity by pigeonholing customers.

The solution for the customers' need for flexibility doesn't come from the factory—it is not a *what*-based innovation (it is not a better car), but rather a *how*-based one. The mobility contract presents an idealized offering—one that removes the constraints of the inflexible product we sell and offers the consumer the flexibility of driving a vehicle that fits the usage occasion, in twenty-four-hour blocks. Eventually, as happens with many radical ideas, the mobility contract did not see the light of day in the form that Reitzle envisaged (he left the company before the idea could leave the drawing board). But the urban automobile market has clearly moved in the direction that Reitzle foresaw: greater flexibility of ownership, with the rapid growth of car-sharing and metered-leasing companies such as Cambio, Getaround, and Zipcar, is now one of the fastest-growing value propositions in the automotive market. The opportunity of a truly global or national mobility solution offered by a car company remains open, although as Reitzle pointed out, it requires a formidable infrastructure that would allow delivery of any vehicle anywhere. Such an infrastructure is not unlike the one Ford, the parent company of PAG, possesses with its wide range of products and thousands of rental locations around the world in its Hertz car rental business.

Highlighting Risks

The second question for uncovering opportunities for downstream competitive advantage is to enumerate the risks incurred by the customer in doing business with a company. We already saw risk reduction in action with the Sainsbury wine example in a consumer setting. Let's switch gears and consider an example in a business-to-business setting. MasterBuilders is a supplier of chemical additives for the construction industry. Its additives, which are blended into the concrete mix at construction sites, give the concrete various properties, including lowered brittleness, or lower sensitivity to temperature variations. But these additives account for a small percentage of the value of the concrete mix. What's more, the additives are seen as a commodity and often as an afterthought by the buyers, the construction contractors. The contractors usually have multiple sites on the go at any given time, and each site prepares its own mix. Purchases of additives are based on competitive bids submitted to the contractors, and buying decisions are often based on minor price differences.

One large customer, a cement contractor with over two hundred site locations, signed a contract with MasterBuilders and then, as was typical, had site managers at each location independently order and maintain inventory to suit their local construction requirements. But local site managers did not always accurately anticipate their needs. Last-minute orders and stock-outs were common and extremely expensive to serve. A half- or quarter-load truck made the trip to cover an emergency order. These last-minute orders were also very expensive to the customer: construction at the site could stall for lack of additives. One solution might have been for MasterBuilders to charge more for delivery or charge for emergency deliveries, passing on the added transportation costs to the customer and encouraging site managers to place large and timely orders. But for the customer, the cost of a stock-out was already very high. Making it marginally higher by charging a penalty was not going to create the right incentives. It would not solve the problem, and it would make MasterBuilders uncompetitive and even unpopular with its customers.

Instead, the company recognized that the primary risk the customer faced was that a stock-out could bring the project to a halt. For the lack of a minor additive, expensive machinery and labor would idle, adding to potential time and cost overruns on the project. Recognition of this larger impact of the risk of an additive stock-out uncovered an opportunity. MasterBuilders began work on a solution to reduce, not increase, the customer's risk.

At no cost to the customer, each construction site was fitted with a storage tank for additives. The tank and its contents remained the property of MasterBuilders until the additives were consumed by the project. The storage tanks were equipped with remote monitoring that reported directly to MasterBuilders the remaining level of the additive. Using the inventory levels and implied usage rates, the small, geographically dispersed orders delivered at infrequent and sometimes unplanned intervals were replaced by large trucks that followed a planned delivery route. This new system offered the customer considerable new value, the most significant of which was the elimination of the risk of stock-outs.

Additional savings were achieved by reducing the overall level of inventory, slashing order and payment processing, and cutting the hassle of inventory management. MasterBuilders, for its part, had financed the program, including the silos, the relaying equipment, and the inventory tracking system, entirely through the savings achieved in the trucking of chemicals. But cost savings alone were not the goal of this project. The company now had satisfied customers. A competitor offering a lower price was unlikely to overcome the risk-reduction advantage that MasterBuilders had built.

MasterBuilders gained an advantage by asking what risks the customer was taking in buying from the company. What made this solution particularly effective was that competitors had not yet asked the question. And if or when they did, it would take them considerable time to develop the systems to deliver a similar risk-lowering solution. In the meantime, MasterBuilders enjoyed a competitive lead and lower customer price sensitivity in an otherwise commodity industry.

Why Don't They Buy from Us?

The third question you can ask when creating value in the downstream is why potential customers don't buy from you. Potential customers are those that by any definition of the target market should be buying from you, but are currently either staying away from the product category as a whole or buying from your competitors. Asking why they do not buy from you, and framing the question in terms of the possible costs and risks that prevent them from buying, helps you develop targeted solutions that are often much more cost-effective than offering price discounts or other inducements to attract them. Consider the case of Hyundai in the depths of the Great Recession of 2008–2009.

At the start of the deep recession in the fall of 2008, as the economy faltered and future job prospects for millions of employed Americans looked uncertain, automobile sales crashed through the floor. Consumers were delaying purchases of consumer durables, in particular cars, until they had better visibility of where the economy was going, and of their own job prospects. The effects on automobile companies were severe. GM and Chrysler's long-term financial problems resurfaced with a vengeance, and both companies sought government bailouts. Hyundai, which had a slew of models targeted at customers in the lower-income segments, was particularly hard hit as the subprime mortgage crisis peaked. The company's US sales dropped 37 percent.[1]

As demand plunged, the immediate response of most car companies was to slash prices and roll out discounts in the form of cash-back offers and other dealer-lot incentives. Hyundai, too, considered these, but eventually took a different approach: it asked why customers were not buying. The answer from its customers was resoundingly, "Because the risk of buying now, when the parlous state of the economy means I could lose my job at any time, is simply too high. If I finance the purchase or lease the car and then have to return the car when I lose my job, my credit rating will take a hit."

Instead of offering a price reduction, Hyundai devised a risk-reduction guarantee to target consumer concerns directly: if you lose your job or income within a year of buying the car, you can return the car with no penalty to your credit rating. Labeled the Hyundai Assurance, the guarantee directly addressed the buyer's primary reason for holding back on the purchase of a new vehicle. The program was launched in January 2009. Hyundai sales that month nearly doubled, while the rest of the industry's sales declined 37 percent, the biggest January drop since 1963.

Hyundai sold more vehicles than Chrysler, which has four times as many dealers. It would not have been very difficult for competitors to match Hyundai's offer of the guarantee. Yet they didn't. They continued to slash prices and offer cash incentives.

Uncovering costs and risks and then reducing them creates value for customers and pays off for sellers. In the PAG example, the costs to the customer were hidden: the cost of owning a particular type of car is the forgoing of other types of cars. But because hidden costs tend to be difficult to uncover, they present an opportunity: because your competitors are less likely to uncover those costs, you can find a basis for differentiation that customers value. MasterBuilders and Hyundai focused on the risks inherent in the buying or the consuming of the product. In my experience, managers often overlook the buyers' risks, even when the risks are not hidden. Risks tend to be less tangible and less apparent than costs. But as a seller, your payoff in addressing customer risks tends to be high for two reasons. First, when you directly address the reason for buying or not buying rather than attempting to offer a price discount, you are able to maintain your margins. Second, competitors are less likely to see the risks and do something to reduce them. Hyundai's competitors, for example, did not follow its example of offering a no-penalty return policy.

It may sound paradoxical, but each of the examples we've seen also shows that by reducing the customers' costs and risks, you can actually increase the price they are willing to pay, even in highly price-competitive markets.

Systematic Cost and Risk Reduction

In companies where the upstream weighs heavily on decisions and strategy, the absence of systematic processes, organizational structures, and budgets for downstream innovation is often an ad hoc endeavor, driven by the initiative of an enterprising manager or team. Making the process more systematic would help companies recognize and seize downstream sources of competitive advantage, provide a way of breaking down the task of downstream innovation into manageable steps, reduce the uncertainty of investments in downstream innovation, and yield sustainable forms of competitive advantage. What would such a process look like?

Let's begin with an examination of customer behavior. The following questions are designed to help you analyze the buying process to uncover the costs that customers incur in doing business with you.[2] Ask yourself how your customers do the following tasks:

- Realize they need a product like yours.
- Come to know about your product.
- Obtain more information about your product (and those of your competitors).
- Test or sample your product.
- Compare your product or offer with those of competitors.
- Narrow down the set of alternatives from which to buy. Are you in that smaller set?
- Pick your product from that smaller set. (Or, why does the customer not pick your product?)
- Take delivery of your product and unpack it.
- Dispose of the packaging materials.
- Set up the product for use.
- Use and enjoy the product. (How does the customer use the product beyond its prescribed or anticipated uses?)
- Extract the benefits for which they bought the product.
- Pay for the product.
- Store the product.
- Maintain the product.

- Upgrade the product.
- Discard the spent product.
- Find your product again if they liked it.
- Tell others about your product.

Similarly, consider questions the customers might ask themselves about the risks of doing business with you:

- Can I trust the seller's promises?
- Will the product perform as expected? Will it do what is promised?
- What are the side effects?
- Is the product dangerous in any way?
- Will I be able to use it successfully?
- Will I lose money on the purchase price? Can I afford it?
- Will it cost a lot to maintain?
- Is the product compatible with other products I use?
- Will it depreciate? If so, how quickly?
- Will the product become obsolete?
- Will I run out of the product or its refills?
- Will the product still be available when I need it next?
- Will the seller be around for repair and maintenance?
- Is the product socially acceptable? What does my use of the product signal about me to others?
- What are the risks to the environment?
- What are the regulations surrounding the use and disposal of this product?

- Will my bosses in the organization agree with my decision? Does it fit company policy, history, culture, and implicit agreements?
- Will I look good and be a success by choosing this product?

These questions highlight the customer's uncertainty about any purchase. Keep in mind that your customers buy your products despite this uncertainty or because they have found some way of reducing or living with this uncertainty. Whatever their solution, if you can find a way to reduce uncertainty more efficiently, you can create value for the customer.

Answers to the cost and risk questions uncover the effort the customer expends and the risks the customer takes to extract the benefits you promise them from your products. Each cost and each risk reduces the value the customers get from their interaction with you, and each reduction in costs or risks that you can deliver increases that value. In the Sainsbury, PAG, MasterBuilders, and Hyundai examples in this chapter, each company picked one point of pain—one critical cost or one risk borne by the customer—and reduced it to create a new form of value for the customer. But despite the effectiveness of the solutions they developed, each innovation is still ad hoc—it tackles a single point of pain. And even if the solution yields a successful innovation, there is no guarantee that a stream of innovations will ensue. A downstream innovation machine would require a business to conduct a similar exercise more systematically and on a larger scale, covering all of the customer touch points and potentially unleashing a gusher of downstream innovation. This process begins with a systematic audit of the costs and risks borne by your customers. The objective of such an audit is to uncover as many value-creation opportunities as possible.

Take, for example, the purchase and use of servers and desktop and laptop computers by large organizations such as corporate customers. Clearly, the steps in the transaction involve many different people, teams, and units within both the buying and the selling organization. In table 2-1, I've simplified the process to five touch points: prepurchase (information search and evaluation of alternatives), purchase (including

TABLE 2-1

Touch points, customer costs, and customer risks

	Touch point				
	Prepurchase	Purchase, delivery, installation	Usage	Maintenance	Disposal, renewal, repurchase
***Costs* incurred by our customers**					
***Risks* incurred by our customers**					

delivery and installation), usage, maintenance, and disposal (including renewal and repurchase). This inventory of touch points can be as detailed as you think necessary, as long as it allows you to describe the costs and risks at a level where they can be tackled and reduced.

Let's follow the typical customer's buying behavior at each of the touch points to uncover their costs and risks. At the prepurchase stage, the buying organization's IT department establishes internal requirements and specifications both for centrally used computers and for each department. Salespeople's computers are equipped and configured differently from those for HR, and those in turn are different from machines bound for accounting or production. Each department's hardware and software requirements are assessed and specified.

The IT department then searches the web catalogs of suppliers, talks to the salespeople of the computer vendors, establishes a short list, obtains quotes, picks a supplier, and places an order. A few weeks later, the computers begin to arrive at the IT department, where they are unpacked. Common enterprise software as well as departmental software is loaded, and the computers are taken to the end users. IT next sees the computers when repairs and maintenance issues arise. These are not insignificant. It turns out that over their lifetime, computers cost the company at least twice as much as the initial purchase price. This cost includes the outlays for the IT department's interventions for installation, service, repair, troubleshooting, software updates, and so on.

Over 80 percent of Dell's computer sales are to corporate customers. The company has a deep understanding of the prepurchase, purchase, use, maintenance, and disposal touch points with these organizations. Over the years, Dell has developed innovative ways of addressing customers' costs and risks at each touch point.

At the prepurchase phase, Dell develops customized web catalogs, which it calls Premier Pages, for each company and, often, for each department within that company. Users in the buying organization can call up their specific Premier Page, key in their employee code, and browse a catalog of hardware, software, and options available to them. They do not see any extraneous information—for example, they do not have to sift through lists of options not available to their department—the preselection is done for them, saving users time and effort. The catalog can also keep track of each user's budget, so the user can place orders directly on the page.

Rather than have the enterprise and departmental software installed by IT during the unpacking phase, the programs are preloaded during production, on Dell's assembly line. This automated step takes forty-five seconds, as opposed to the hour or more it would take IT in the buying company to laboriously customize each machine.

The computer is generally delivered directly to the user. IT does not need to receive, store, unpack, customize, or deliver the machine. This is a significant cost savings for the buying organization.

Dell also rethought the usage phase of its customer interaction. Troubleshooting, updates, and software repairs are done by Dell over the Internet, whenever possible, minimizing the IT department's costs of intervention.

Finally, Dell encourages its customers to engage in a three- to five-year planning cycle for IT needs. This process includes a discussion of the renewal of the IT infrastructure and machines, as well as the recycling of the old machines. Planning over five years reduces both the customers' costs (through redeployment, planned obsolescence, and management of the total cost of ownership) and the risks of being caught off guard by expansion needs or new technology. The approach also provides Dell with a stable planning horizon for account planning, staffing, and capacity utilization. And, in a fickle computer market, it provides a reason for the customer to stay with Dell.

Through these cost and risk reduction initiatives, Dell creates value for buying organizations well beyond the product. In an industry where the technology and products of the larger computer manufacturers are at parity, Dell may not sell better computers, but by reducing customers' costs and risks, it sells computers better.

Identifying Innovation Opportunities

Identification of the costs and risks that your customers bear at each touch point is a first step. Next you need to consider whether you can address those costs and risks more efficiently than your customers can. Two questions will help you at this stage. First, are there scale efficiencies in aggregating the costs and risks? Very simply, the question means this: does the per-unit cost or risk go down when you pool it or do it on a scale the customer can't? For example, Dell automates the installation of software on the assembly line, accomplishing in forty-five seconds what the customer labors to do in one hour. Similarly, insurance companies would not exist if it were not more efficient to pool risk than to carry it individually. Many costs and risks associated with each stage of the customer interaction present similar opportunities for achieving efficiencies through pooling and aggregation. These are opportunities to create downstream competitive advantage.

The second, related question will reveal whether you can address the costs and risks more efficiently than your customers: where in the value chain does it make the most sense for those costs and risks to be addressed? Take a simple example of a cost question: who should carry the cost of holding inventory, the manufacturer or the distributor? Another way of asking the questions is, should the seller extend credit to the buyer, and if so, how many days of credit? If the number of days of credit is generally settled through negotiation between the buyer and the seller, the answer should largely be based on the relative cost of working capital for the manufacturer versus the distributor. If the manufacturer can borrow more cheaply than the distributor, the manufacturer should offer to bear the cost of carrying the inventory and negotiate, in exchange, better shelf positioning, greater push, cooperative advertising, or anything else that the distributor can do more efficiently than the manufacturer and that the manufacturer values.

A similar logic applies when you determine where you should locate risk. Consider a typical negotiation between a manufacturer of branded toothpaste and its largest customer, a retail chain. The manufacturer is launching a new type of toothpaste. Test market results have found that consumers in the target segment love the new product and find it superior to their current brand on practically every dimension that matters to them. The target segment is large, and the manufacturer's projections indicate that a good number of consumers will switch to the new product at a reasonable price, making it potentially very profitable for both the manufacturer and the retailer. So the manufacturer attempts to convince the retailer to allocate shelf space to this new toothpaste. The retailer, however, is reticent. Arguing that the toothpaste category is already very crowded and that the well-established brands have good margins and good turnover, the retailer sees no reason to rock the boat. After a lot of back and forth, the retailer agrees to take on only a small initial order as a trial. But the manufacturer knows from past experience that unless the retailer allocates a critical mass of shelf space at launch, the product is doomed to fail. The manufacturer thus faces the challenge of trying to convince the retailer to place a full order and to allocate sufficient shelf-facing to give the new toothpaste a chance. The last thing the manufacturer wants is to spend large sums on launch advertising to drive consumers into stores where they can't find the product because the retailer gave it too little shelf space or did not order enough of it.

Still, the retailer continues to see the new-product launch as a risky proposition. After all, the grocery business experiences a very high rate of new-product failure (over 80 percent of new products introduced fail to meet the revenue hurdle after twelve months).[3] The retailer is thus acutely sensitive to the risks of introducing new products. Retailers can be left holding inventory that does not move and that cannot easily be disposed of, and they risk the opportunity cost of allocating shelf space to a loser when they could have allocated it to a winner. At this point in the negotiations, most manufacturers offer the retailer higher margins, large listing fees, facing fees, and other monetary inducements to take on the new product. This typical negotiation is hardly unique to the toothpaste category or the grocery trade—it plays out, in some form, in almost every industry.

But consider what just happened. The manufacturer misread the retailer's reticence as a negotiating ploy or a request for larger margins or lower costs. In fact, the gulf between the manufacturer and the retailer arises because of very different perceptions of risk: the retailer sees the risk of the new product introduction as far greater than the manufacturer does. Given this asymmetrical perceived risk, the appropriate manufacturer response to the retailer should not be an offer to reduce the retailer's cost, but rather to absorb any risk associated with the launch. In other words, if the manufacturer is so certain of the product's success and sees it as much less risky than does the retailer, the manufacturer should shoulder the risk. For example, the manufacturer could offer to take back any unsold inventory if the product does not sell at benchmark levels. Or it could offer to compensate the retailer for margin lost if and only if the product does not move. Instead, by offering a large listing fee and by discounting the product, the manufacturer sacrifices future profits to overcome a onetime hurdle of getting the product on the shelf. The retailer might demand the same high margins for future shipments, even if the product is very successful. Mislocating risk in the value chain can prove costly in the long term.

Operational and Informational Solutions

Try this exercise at work. Gather your team, and fill in each of the cells in table 2-1, listing the costs and risks your customers incur at each buying stage. Then ask how you can reduce these. You will find that there are two types of solutions to reduce customers' costs and risks: operational and informational. Operational solutions tend to be about delivering the product at the right time and place and in the right format and making it easy for customers to buy, consume, and dispose of the product. Examples we've seen include Coca-Cola's vending machines, MasterBuilders' vendor-managed inventory system, Dell's customization of software on computers on the assembly line, and Dell's direct delivery to end users in the buying organization. All of these operational solutions reduced costs and risks. Each creates tremendous customer value through operations designed to fit how customers buy and consume your product. These types of opportunities for operational innovation tend to be difficult to uncover but relatively simple to implement once you look for them on the grid in table 2-1.

The second way to reduce customers' costs and risks involves information and the networks through which information flows. Sainsbury's reduction of consumer costs and risks of wine selection, Janssen Pharmaceutica's development of a serious video game, and the Hyundai Assurance plan are examples of harnessing the power of information to serve the customer. Much of the remainder of this book is about two types of information that create downstream competitive advantage: (1) information that sellers use to map markets and customer networks, and (2) information that buyers use to understand sellers and the market. Part 2 of this book is devoted to the first type of informational competitive advantage, and part 3 is about the second type. But before we get there, the next chapter will take a closer look at the idea of competitive advantage in the downstream.

The Cost and Risk Checklist

✓ Have you mapped your customers' information search process for your products? Where do they incur the most costs? What types of risks are they trying to reduce? Can you uncover consumer behavior using the list of questions in "Systematic Cost and Risk Reduction," above?

- ✓ How do consumers decide which products to buy in the product category in which you play? How do they decide when to buy, how much to buy, and at what price to buy?
- ✓ Which expert sources of information and advice do your customers rely on before they make a purchase in your product category?
- ✓ Can you design your communication, branding, and delivery to reduce the customers' costs and risks?

3. Seizing the Downstream Advantage

Companies that tilt downstream are not just escaping the barren upstream playing fields; they are seizing new and valuable sources of competitive advantage. But what exactly is downstream competitive advantage, and why is it different from and better than upstream competitive advantage? In the previous chapters, we've looked at a number of examples of downstream innovation, that is, new forms of value that create competitive advantage. Let's build on those to examine what makes downstream advantage unique.

Strategy is the means by which a business entity seeks to outperform competitors. In other words, strategy is a quest for a wrinkle in the market that will allow a firm to generate returns greater than those of its competitors. In efficient markets, it is not easy for firms to find lasting sources of competitive advantage. Rivals are quick to locate and replicate sources of advantage and iron out the wrinkles. Still, some firms do build formidable businesses that consistently churn out healthy, above-average returns. If firms are bundles of resources, knowledge, capabilities, and other assets, then competition between firms is a competition between different and differentiated bundles. No two firms are identical. The thesis of *Tilt* is that since not all parts of the resource bundle contribute equally to lasting competitive advantage, the strategic key is to find or develop aspects of the bundle that do.

A successful tilt strategy, as we have seen, groups your firm's resources and activities into two buckets: upstream or downstream. Companies seeking a wrinkle to exploit in the upstream tend to home in on advantages such as new products, technologies, features, low-cost sources of supply, and efficient production processes. Downstream sources of competitive advantage, in contrast, reside in your knowledge of, and your links with, your customer base and their knowledge of you. Let's examine why these two types of competitive advantage are so different.

Upstream and downstream sources of competitive advantage differ in their locus, of course, but they also differ on a number of other dimensions. Table 3-1 summarizes these differences, whose implications we will now explore.

TABLE 3-1

Differences in upstream and downstream competitive advantage

	Upstream	Downstream
Locus of competitive advantage	Internal: resides inside the company, in its assets (including intangible ones like patents), resources, skills, processes, and knowledge	External: resides in the marketplace and in the company's linkages to customers and marketplace networks
Types and sources of competitive advantage	Access to low-cost sources of supply; efficiencies in production or logistics; scale; proprietary technology, patents; product and R&D capabilities; people; procedures; and organizational structure and culture	Market information; customer relationships and loyalty; market presence and influence over customers' criteria of purchase; control of pace of market change; customers' perceptions of the company and its brands.
Basis of customer value	Cost leadership or differentiation	Cost and risk reduction
Innovation	New products, technologies, and R&D, often represented by patent banks; new-product pipelines; and new-product development systems	New ways of interacting with customers; cost and risk reduction; market-based innovation
Sustainability of competitive advantage	Competitive advantage erodes as competitors catch up, imitate, replicate, or leapfrog product and technology innovations	Competitive advantage is *accumulative*: can grow with time, experience, and accumulation of information, e.g., network effects

Prisoners of Their Own Walls

Upstream competitive advantage tends to be located inside the firm. In trying to seize upstream competitive advantage, companies scramble to lock up sources of supply (e.g., exploration rights for oil companies) or achieve efficiencies in production or logistics (e.g., install radio frequency identification systems), build large-scale production infrastructure, develop and patent proprietary technology, hone R&D capabilities, assemble high-performance teams, build lean and efficient organizational structures, and develop a unique culture. Common to all of these endeavors is the idea of building unique assets or capabilities, then constructing a wall around them. The purpose of the wall is to foster and maintain the advantage—to prevent the source of competitive advantage from leaking out to competitors and the rest of the world. You can tell which aspects of the firm's internal functioning it considers a source of competitive advantage by how well protected these aspects are. If the company believes its production processes are its source of competitive advantage, plant visits are strictly controlled, security around its factories is airtight, and new products never leak until they are launched. If the firm believes its R&D is its source of competitive advantage, bank-level security surrounds its research labs, and armies of lawyers surround its patents. And if it deems its people are its competitive advantage, as many Silicon Valley firms do, you will find cozy work environments, catered lunches, state-of-the-art gyms, yoga studios, nap nooks, sabbaticals, and flexible work hours. At Facebook, the company will even do your laundry for you.[1]

Yet, over time, those walls and protection mechanisms can have a pernicious effect: they can keep the external world out. In the extreme, companies become obsessed with what is inside their walls and remain oblivious to the outside world of customers, complementors, channel members, and competitors. In one possible evolutionary trajectory for such companies, their interactions with markets and, in particular, customers can become circumscribed, highly scripted, stultified, and limited to transactions where product is transferred in exchange for money. The companies' ability to listen to the market and respond to its changing needs withers because they are focused on protecting their internal sources of competitive advantage. They obsess about producing more because each unit brings in more revenue and a good margin. This increased revenue allows them to invest in a larger factory or more of any other internal advantage they believe makes them successful. These investments raise their upstream fixed costs, so they now need to sell more. Volume becomes the primary imperative. The upstream focus becomes self-reinforcing. The market may even buy more for a while. But in their internal focus, upstream players eventually neglect to ask why the customer is buying their product and, in particular, why the customer is buying from them rather than from their competitors. At the logical conclusion of this trajectory, they find themselves enclosed inside the walls they erected.

Breaking Out of the Walls

Downstream competitive advantage, in contrast, does not reside on the premises. It cannot be locked up at night. Its locus is in the marketplace, in the company's linkages with the market, in company interactions with customers, in the company's understanding of the marketplace, and in customers' behavior and loyalty stemming from their perceptions of the company and the marketplace. A brand reputation, for example, is not located inside the walls of the company, but resides in the minds of consumers. Its effects are felt in the marketplace and are evident in the behavior of customers. A brand—a dispersed, market-based asset that resides in the minds of millions of customers—is only nominally owned by the company.

In a simple experiment by researchers at the Stanford School of Medicine, sixty-three preschoolers ranging in age from 3.5 to 5.4 years tasted five pairs of identical foods, including baby carrots, and either milk or apple juice.[2] One set of foods was wrapped in McDonald's packaging, while the other identical set was placed in plain packaging. Of the sixty-three kids, 23 percent said they preferred the carrots that were presented to them in the plain packaging, 23 percent said there was no difference between the two, and a whopping 54 percent preferred the carrots in the McDonald's packaging. The results for milk or apple juice were even more striking, with 61 percent preferring their beverages in McDonald's packaging. Unsurprisingly, the effect was positively related to the number of television sets at home. The greater the number of TV sets the child had at home, the greater the preference for food in McDonald's packaging. From an early age, consumers experience the world through brands. Their choices and behavior are influenced by brands. Brands are a powerful downstream competitive advantage because they are embedded in consumers' minds. Upstream-focused companies looking for tangible assets may consider their trademarks tangible proof that their brands reside on their premises. They may even litigate to protect the trademarks from competitors that try to usurp them. But if consumer perceptions of the brand, or consumers' product preferences, change over time, trademarks offer little protection and are of little value. The source of competitive advantage resides in the marketplace, in the minds of consumers. Players that tilt downstream recognize that their brands are intangible and widely dispersed.

Brands are not the only marketplace asset. Consider a company such as Netflix, which has revolutionized the movie rental business and spawned dozens of imitators. Netflix remains ahead of its competitors, thanks to the systems it has created to harness and facilitate the flow of marketplace information. It left its main bricks-and-mortar rival, Blockbuster, in the dust not just because Netflix is an online operation that dispenses with the costs of maintaining a physical infrastructure of stores and shelves. Rather, Netflix's advantage is the information that it gathers from its customer network: customers rate the movies they watch, and Netflix uses those ratings to recommend movies to other customers. The system connects the preferences of its viewers to those of other viewers. By building these marketplace connections and offering new ways of capturing, analyzing, and disseminating information, Netflix stays ahead of its competition. The marketplace information that it has harnessed is a downstream asset—Netflix has simply built the channels through which it flows better to its customers. The information that reaches customers through these channels reduces customers' risk of picking a movie they won't like. For this, they keep coming back to Netflix, even after it decided one day in 2012 to raise its prices by 60 percent.

The Market Is the Ultimate Test

Even upstream sources of competitive advantage must ultimately meet a market test: do customers value the lower cost or the differentiation that is produced by the upstream advantage? Under a low-cost strategy, a company can make products more efficiently or more cheaply than competitors and sell the goods at a price similar to that offered by competitors, the result being higher returns. Or a company can make products more cheaply *and* sell them more cheaply and, in doing so, sell more of them, again receiving higher returns. Where differentiation rather than lower cost is the source of competitive advantage, a company invests in making its products better. And if some customers do indeed find the products to be superior, they may be willing to pay a higher price, providing the firm with a higher return.

In a nutshell, those are the strategic options available to upstream players. As a result, their efforts to renew their competitive advantage—their innovation efforts—focus on either product innovation or process innovation. They either build better products or find more efficient and otherwise better ways to make those products.

Downstream players, in contrast, seek competitive advantage by reducing customers' costs and risks. Their superior returns are the result of customers' willingness either to pay more or to buy more from the downstream player because of lower costs and risks. As we have seen, Dell and MasterBuilders gain both customer loyalty and increased pricing power by addressing customers' costs and risks; Hyundai reduces customers' risk so it does not have to offer the price discounts that are crushing its competitors.

As we will see throughout this book, the sources of competitive advantage from the downstream are less prone to erosion than are sources of competitive advantage in the upstream. Competitors are quicker to replicate, neutralize, and commoditize upstream competitive advantage than they are to do the same thing with downstream advantage. Later in the book, after exploring how firms can build downstream competitive advantage, we will learn why this type of advantage is more sustainable. But first, part 2 urges us to develop a big-picture perspective of the entire marketplace network of customers, suppliers, competitors, and complementors. In part 3, we will go on a deep dive inside the customer's mind to explore and understand the competitive playing field that exists there.

The Competitive Advantage Checklist

Looking at the descriptions in table 3-1 in this chapter, consider the following questions:

- ✓ Are your sources of competitive advantage internal to the firm or external? Can your competitive advantage be said to reside inside the firm or in the marketplace?
- ✓ What is the basis of your differentiation with respect to competitors: is it cost leadership, product differentiation, or risk and cost reduction for customers?
- ✓ When you think of innovation, do you think in terms of new products, or do you look at innovation more broadly, in terms of new forms of value for customers? Do you find yourself defending patents and products rather than brands and market positions?
- ✓ How sustainable is your competitive advantage? Does it erode quickly; do competitors catch up too easily? Is your differentiation stable, or is it rapidly replicated by competitors?

Part Two

The Perch

Mapping Market Networks

4. Seeing New Value in Your Customers

No matter what business you are in, you know things about your customers that they don't know and can't find out on their own—but that they would value immensely if you would share with them. In this chapter, I will describe how this unexploited knowledge may be your firm's greatest and most undervalued asset, how it is often hidden in plain sight, and how it is the source of unique insights that only you possess.

Regardless of how competent and smart they are, your customers operate within one big constraint: they find it difficult to transcend the narrow boundaries of the range of their own experience. If they are business-to-business customers, they rarely see what happens beyond the confines of their own business, the limits of the relationships with their own suppliers and customers, and transactions in their own markets. If you are in a business-to-consumer industry, your customers rarely get a glimpse of the entire marketplace. In either case, customers almost never see the aggregate picture or patterns that emerge when you can simultaneously see an entire industry, an entire customer base, or an entire market.

Unlike each of your customers, you have access to the big picture and can see different things in the marketplace than what your customers can. You can see problems that are likely to arise, because they have arisen elsewhere; you can see solutions to problems that plague a particular customer or subgroup of customers, because you have seen solutions successfully implemented elsewhere. Just as importantly, you might know what won't work, because you have seen it fail elsewhere. And finally, you can see patterns they can't see, because you're looking at the entire market all at once, and this different perspective yields unique insight. But the big picture is an abstract concept, so before we get into a description and a definition, let's work through an example.

A Booming Business?

The big picture was used to great effect by the Australian division of ICI explosives. Some years ago, ICI was a company stuck in a commodity trap, mired in intense price competition with several other similar firms selling explosives that were used by quarries to blast solid rock into pieces of roughly equal size. The quarries' primary business was to produce as much similarly sized rock as possible to sell to their customers in the landscaping and construction industries. Since the explosives sold by the competing suppliers were nearly identical, the quarries chose suppliers almost exclusively on the basis of price. In this respect, the competitive pressures in this business were not so different from many commodity businesses in other industries.

ICI's profitability depended on retaining customers, and keeping customers in this environment was not easy. Small price reductions by competitors could pry customers loose. There were no major penalties for switching, such as changeover costs, retooling, or a learning curve necessary to use competitors' explosives. Changing suppliers was almost as easy as lighting a match. This meant that for explosives sellers, every bid mattered and every bit of price difference on each bid helped.

But at a strategic level, ICI recognized that if it wanted respite from the intense competition and profitability beyond the minimal margins of a commodity business, it had to entirely rethink its business approach. It had to step back from the natural desire to win each bid and had instead looked for the bigger picture.

If you had asked ICI executives at the time (or any of ICI's competitors, for that matter) what business they were in, the obvious, natural, and inadequate answer would have been "the business of selling explosives." Like most companies, ICI focused on the product it was selling. But in rethinking its business, the company for the first time attempted to address a different question: what are the customers buying?

With this change in point of view, ICI realized that none of its customers were particularly interested in explosives other than as a means of creating broken rock. Not surprisingly, the quarries' primary concern was to produce broken rock to well-defined specifications while minimizing the cost of their input. They saw no reason to pay more for ICI's or any other company's explosives. Standard marketing responses to this dilemma—attempts to educate the quarries on the fine differences that made ICI's explosives superior, empowering and motivating the frontline salespeople to build relationships with buyers, changing package format, offering different pricing terms—fell on deaf ears or were easily replicated by competitors.

For the quarries, haggling over the price of explosives was a necessary but tedious distraction from their real task: breaking rock. And breaking rock is not as easy as it sounds. If the quarries failed to design the initial blast perfectly or to use the correct amount of explosives in the correct placement, much of the rock that resulted would be too large or too small for their customers to use. Too large, and the quarries would have to break up the rock again, a time-consuming and expensive effort. Too small, and the customer wouldn't take the output.

As up to twenty parameters affect the performance of a blast, a lot can go wrong. The literal profile of the rock face; the location, depth, and diameter of the bored holes; and even the weather can alter the required amounts of explosives used and the way they are laid. Mess up this complex formula often enough, and your profits crumble into dust and get blown away by the wind.

The Big-Picture Opportunity

In this dilemma, ICI saw its opportunity. If the company limited itself to defining its business as selling explosives, competing on price, and defining customer efficiency in terms of cost reductions, there was no way for ICI to stand out. But if the company used its view of the big picture as an advantage, it could develop a whole new strategy, with new sources of competitive advantage and a new, differentiated offering.

Managers began by asking the important initial question: what are the hidden costs and risks that ICI's customers incur when they buy and use ICI products? The company concluded that its customers' greatest fears revolved around the risk of errors during blasts and the cost of correcting the blast output when errors occurred. Thinking more deeply from the vantage point of its customers, ICI realized that there was also an unspoken anxiety about storing, transporting, and handling the explosives correctly and without accidents. At this point the company recognized something that had been true all along for the quarries: these costs and risks far outweighed the differences in the price of the explosives between competing suppliers. If ICI could systematically reduce even just some of these risks, it would be providing significant new value for the quarries—far in excess of any price reduction ICI or any of its competitors could offer.

ICI had discovered that all of its customers faced the same limiting factor: their expertise in blasting was limited, because of the narrow range of conditions within which they operated. This drawback, however, did not apply to ICI, as the company monitored a significant number of blasts made by many quarries, in a wide variety of geological and climatic conditions. The problem, but also the glaring opportunity, was that to date, neither ICI nor any of its competitors or the customers had systematically assembled and analyzed the data.

When ICI's engineers culled data on conditions and outcomes from hundreds of blasts, across a wide range of quarries, they saw something that had never been seen before: patterns that helped explain blast outcomes. ICI now had something that each quarry, acting independently, lacked: a pool of data reflecting a broad base of experience and covering a wide range of conditions. Using empirical models and experimentation, ICI developed strategies and procedures that greatly reduced the uncertainty that, until then, had gone hand in hand with blasting rock. The company could now predict and control the size of the rock that would result from a blast under specific conditions.

ICI then faced a strategic choice. It could continue to sell explosives, offering its new expertise as an added service. This approach would give the business a clear edge, but would also keep the company in the same orbit as its competitors. The approach would also present others in the industry with a clear target, one that said, "Copy this." So, instead of following that path, ICI made a bolder move and began writing contracts for the outcome that customers wanted: broken rock produced to spec. It billed its customers for the outcome of the blasts, promising them that the result of the explosion would be a certain percentage of broken rock falling within a prespecified size range.

The redefinition of the contract meant that ICI no longer sold a commodity. Instead, it was in the business of selling a highly differentiated value proposition created by the application of engineering expertise, marketing savvy, and strategic acumen. Each of these elements came together in assembling a big-picture view of the marketplace from pieces of data from hundreds of blasts at dozens of quarries.[1]

Even more importantly, the competitive advantage ICI built on this foundation was difficult for competitors to replicate unless they could gain access to as wide a range of data as ICI's years of experience and variety of clients provided. Finally, ICI's special kind of competitive advantage had an interesting characteristic: it was accumulative. The more blasts ICI conducted, the more data it collected. And the more refined its models and blasts became, the further ahead it pulled from its competitors.

As part of everyday working life, you come into contact with a variety of customers, each with unique needs, problems, challenges, desires, and resources. Automatically, just by exposure to this diverse group, you gain a wider range of experience on these issues than any single one of your customers can possibly have. Owing solely to your position in the marketplace, you have a privileged perch that gives you a bird's-eye view of all your customers. This perspective means that you can see the forest while each of your customers can only see the trees.

Of course, using the big picture does not imply that you should divulge to others the confidential aspects of your customers' business or experience. But as we will see, a lot of nonconfidential information is valuable, or becomes valuable, once you put it together with other bits of information. Information has value not because it is secret, but because it can be assembled with other pieces of information to reveal something new.

In the remainder of this chapter, we will see how firms use their big-picture perspective to reduce customers' costs or risks and are rewarded with customer loyalty, pricing flexibility, or both.[2]

Assembling Puzzles

Imagine that you have five hundred customers, each of whom holds one piece of a five-hundred-piece jigsaw puzzle. While each piece is unique, when assembled the pieces reveal a larger meaning.

Each of your customers possesses information that is akin to a piece or a few pieces of a jigsaw puzzle. They just don't know what to do with it—it is meaningless unless assembled. In most instances, that piece of the puzzle remains forgotten in a drawer, in a database, untouched, and unused because customers fail to realize its possible role in the larger context. Insights from this data never see the light of day. Often, it takes someone from the outside to see the potential of piecing together the puzzle. In the quarry industry, that outsider was ICI, an explosives supplier. In your industry, it could be you. And once you find a way to bring together the five hundred or thousand or several million pieces of information that lie dispersed with customers, you can see patterns you've never seen before. These patterns can help your customers make different and better choices that add value to themselves and to you.

A new big picture can have widespread impact on customer behavior and industry dynamics. The book publishing industry was changed to the core when, in 1895, the now-defunct literary magazine *The Bookman* introduced a monthly ranking of fiction sales. The ranking became the first national best-seller list in the United States.[3] Today, the *New York Times* best-seller list aggregates data on book purchases through many distribution outlets and reflects this big-picture ranking back to readers. It turns out that customers value knowing what others are reading: the lists are powerful drivers of individual reader behavior, boosting sales of books. But before *The Bookman*'s list, readers had no way of seeing the big picture. There are now more than forty national best-seller lists in the fiction category alone, each with its own unique methodology and perspective. Moreover, there are hundreds of best-seller lists for every book category, every music category, and, for that matter, just about any other mass-consumed product. There are daily lists of the top search terms on the search engines such as Yahoo! and Google, the list of the most e-mailed articles in the *New York Times,* and websites such as Reddit that record and disseminate the most popular web pages, the most tweeted tweets, and the most liked Facebook posts. In each of these cases, information about a *group* of customers is aggregated and fed back to *individual* customers. The view of the group is unavailable to the individuals until it is aggregated, but once they know of it, it changes how they behave.

Patterns in the Pixels

Patterns formed by fragmented and distributed pieces of information occur in many surprising places. And it is only now, in the twenty-first century, with the emergence of new measurement, aggregation, and visualization technologies, that we are beginning to see patterns that otherwise went unnoticed, sometimes for centuries.

For thousands of years, farmers, ranchers, herders, and hunters seemingly failed to notice that cattle and deer align in the same direction when grazing in a field, or if they did make this observation, they did not proclaim it very loudly. In 2008, Czech and German zoologists decided to look at Google Earth images of 308 cow pastures and 241 deer localities around the globe. What they noticed was startling: cattle tend to align in a north-south axis, orienting themselves to the earth's magnetic north.[4] As with any startling scientific finding, alternative explanations abounded, including suggestions that the animals were merely maximizing their exposure to the sun or that wind direction would influence the cows' orientation. To rule out these explanations, the scientists examined cattle in pastures located close to electrical power lines. They found that the cows did not align when grazing in proximity of these electrical fields.[5] Instead, the animals were scattered randomly. This lent support to the magnetic-field theory and has excited new interest in explaining animals' magnetic orientation. Yet the alignment phenomenon had apparently gone unnoticed for so long—except, perhaps, by that keen observer of both human and animal behavior, Mark Twain:

> "If fifteen cows is browsing on a hillside, how many of them eats with their heads pointed the same direction?"
>
> "The whole fifteen, mum."
>
> "Well, I reckon you *have* lived in the country. I thought maybe you was trying to hocus me again."[6]

The View from Above

The ability to see the big picture has always been inextricably linked with competitive advantage in strategy. So it is not surprising that strategists are always on the lookout for new technologies that will help them develop a big-picture view that their competitors do not possess. In 1858, Gaspard Félix Tournachon, a jovial, gregarious, inventive, and bohemian Parisian portrait photographer, better known by his nom de plume, Nadar, climbed into a hot-air balloon in the vicinity of Petit Bicêtre, a small village southwest of Paris. He was, like many before and after him, responding to an apparently irresistible human urge: to see ourselves from above, to see the big picture.

The balloon, not in any way special, did not travel far. (In fact, it was tethered to the ground and rose only about 80 meters, or 260 feet, into the air.) But what made that event memorable was that Nadar took with him his photographic equipment, which in those days of wet-plate photography was no small feat. It meant lugging his entire darkroom into the balloon basket with him. Up there, perched above the picturesque Bievre Valley, Nadar became the first person to combine the emerging fields of ballooning and photography, giving birth to the discipline of aerial photography. In time, aerial photography led to innumerable applications in geology, archeology, meteorology, and espionage and to new views of ourselves, including the Apollo 17 picture of the blue planet hanging in space and the ubiquitous Google Earth satellite photographs on your computer screen.

Even back then, Nadar and his contemporaries recognized the value of taking pictures from above. The images offered a unique perspective that quickly became essential to surveying and cartography, and a source of competitive advantage in military strategy and tactics. In fact, within a year of those first photographs, Nadar was offered a lucrative commission by Napoleon III, who wanted a bird's-eye view of enemy troops in his campaign against Italy. Nadar declined the offer because he wasn't in tune with the emperor's politics, but it wasn't long before the inevitable marriage of aerial photography and military strategy was feted. Across the Atlantic, as the US Civil War broke out, Abraham Lincoln appointed Thaddeus Lowe, a chemist and meteorologist, to be the chief aeronaut of the Union Army Balloon Corps. Lowe's aerial reconnaissance spotted and photographed confederate troop movements and helped estimate real-time troop counts, forging a lasting bond between aerial pictures and military strategy.

In the early part of the twentieth century, cameras small enough to be strapped onto carrier pigeons brought aerial reconnaissance into the stealth era. By the end of World War I, aerial photography was a routine part of the war effort. French spooks were said to be developing ten thousand aerial pictures on peak days; the English talked of taking half a million aerial photographs during the war; and the Germans, not to be outdone on this front, claimed they could carpet their entire country with their pictures if they were to set all the aerial war photos side by side. With every subsequent advance in aviation and photographic technology, new applications and new insights have emerged.

Even in the preballoon era, generals on both sides of a battle would perch on high ground to survey the field and command their troops. The view of the entire field gave them insight into their own and the enemy's strategy, which would have been impossible to discern from inside the fray. The maps on which they plotted troop movements were also an attempt to see the big picture—to see the entire playing field at once. But a map is a stylized representation that omits, obscures, or alters much of the real detail to provide a highly simplified model. In contrast, an aerial picture is quasi real-time information that carries as much detail as the photographic resolution will allow. Thanks to these properties, the aerial photograph is an indispensable complement to the map in the field execution of strategy. It allows patterns and changes to be quickly discerned. These properties are important and have direct analogies in business strategy.

The Forest and the Trees

In recent years, information scientists have begun to examine data concerning herd behavior, and not just cattle herds. Several media-monitoring bots and widgets, for example, scan popular social media sites such as Facebook and Twitter to gauge public sentiment around a particular event, topic, product, or brand. For example, in an HP Labs study, social media sentiment was successfully used to predict box office sales of movies. Researchers monitored tweets on about twenty-four movies released between December 2009 and February 2010. The study results suggest that Twitter sentiment is a more accurate way to predict box office sales than other methods such as the popular Hollywood Stock Exchange play-money market (which was specifically created for this purpose). The HP researchers also argue that the method used to create the algorithm could be extended to a variety of other products and services, to predict their commercial success in the early stages of their life cycles.

In another study, three computer scientists investigated whether analyzing public sentiment from a large sample of daily tweets could predict the daily moves of the stock market. Their results confirmed that Twitter feeds do indeed provide a reliable prediction of changes in the Dow Jones Industrial Average.[7] In fact, changes in the public sentiment were shown to predict changes in the index three to four days in advance. Information scientists are looking into whether similar big-picture data can predict election results more accurately than polls can. Another set of studies examined the use of happy words such as "awesome" and "agree" as well as unhappy words such as "annoy" and "afraid" found in five hundred million Tweets, from millions of users in eighty-four countries.[8] One big conclusion: people's moods follow a daily biological rhythm that transcends differences in culture or environment. These types of insights were simply inaccessible even a few years ago, because the data that makes up the big picture was not available, and neither were the measurement, aggregation, and analysis techniques.

Bluefin Labs, for example, is a recent Cambridge, Massachusetts, start-up launched by MIT professor Deb Roy and his doctoral student Michael Fleischman. The company aims to understand how the "Twitter-sphere" (and other social media) respond to television programming and advertising. By analyzing patterns in the tweets that appear in reaction to TV commercials, Bluefin is able to tell advertisers which of their ads had the greatest social media impact and whether that impact was positive or negative. For the first time, advertisers are seeing that the same ad placed in a different programming context with similar ratings can elicit very different audience reactions. Bluefin Labs' social media analysis technology was deemed so valuable, the company was acquired by Twitter in February 2013, and Twitter declared Bluefin's products would not be sold to any new clients.[9]

The implication for business is that a set of developments as big and as far-reaching as Nadar's pioneering combination of photography and ballooning is currently taking place in the way business represents and uses market information. Enormous amounts of data that did not even exist even a few years ago are now routinely generated and captured in the marketplace. Bots are busy collecting and processing the digital trail of billions of crumbs and cookies that Internet surfers leave behind. Telecom carriers analyze call frequency, duration, and timing. Credit card companies know which reward offers are most likely to spur purchase by any given cardholder. Facebook captures data about connections between consumers to find hidden patterns that anticipate consumer behavior. Within seconds of a customer's purchase of a package of Tide at a Walmart store, folks at Procter & Gamble, the makers of Tide, can tell you the size of the package, the price the customer paid for it, whether a coupon was used, and perhaps even the demographic characteristics of the buyer if he or she used a loyalty card. Data from checkout scanners and information from loyalty cards answer the critical marketing questions of who buys what, when, and at what price. These new developments reflect a revolution in the way companies collect and assemble marketplace data. What they do with this data will determine the nature of competitive advantage they establish.

Marketing and the Big Picture

The revolution in marketplace data that took marketing from mass media and mass one-size-fits-all brands and prices to customized one-to-one targeting is currently taking another major turn. A couple of decades ago, when mass marketing still ruled, it was almost impossible, or impossibly expensive, for businesses selling to large numbers of customers to understand and respond to the needs of each individual. As a result, most businesses relied on yearly market-segmentation exercises to help them map and navigate their marketplace. This annual ritual grouped customers into rigid categories and provided a static picture, or map, of their buying habits and behaviors, their likes and dislikes. As on a map, the categories were simplifications and gross generalizations, almost caricatures of customer groups, frozen in time. But even with these flaws, the exercise was valuable because, in the absence of more detailed and real-time information, it allowed marketers to group customers together, to communicate with them efficiently, and to find media that would reach them economically. Toothpaste purchasers were grouped into segments that bought the product for different reasons: for cavity protection, for breath freshening, for teeth whitening, and just for the taste of it.

But in recent years, as individual customer-level and transaction-level data became abundant, the rigid segmentation in old-fashioned mass marketing came to seem archaic. The true fluidity of markets began to be uncovered. It was recognized that the same customer might eat at McDonald's at noon and at a French restaurant in the evening—that occasion, location, and context played a far greater role in customer choices than was realized. At the same time, markets began to move too quickly for annual segmentation to stand the test of time. The caricatures of segments that marketers had drawn in the data were washed away in a flood of new and more detailed customer information about every transaction. As the century turned, and the trickle of data turned into a flood, businesses fell in love with the idea of targeting each individual consumer, not as part of a segment, but as an individual. The marketing game shifted to one-to-one communication and persuasion.

Since then, marketing's holy grail has been to predict what each individual customer will buy next. Targeting the individual customer makes marketing budgets much more efficient and eliminates wasted effort: marketers only target with tailored messages the customers who are most likely to buy or most open to persuasion. An example of how a brand or a retailer might think could be this: "Let's try to address the consumer by name, remember the customer's recent purchases, and remember not to offer 40 percent off the next purchase, because we know that this customer is likely to grab an offer of 20 percent off."

In pursuit of this prize—the next transaction—marketers strive to paint an ever more detailed portrait of each consumer, memorizing the person's media preferences, scrutinizing the shopping habits, and cataloging his or her interests, aspirations, and desires. The result is a detailed, high-resolution close-up of each customer—a close-up that reveals the person's next move.

But in the rush to uncover and target "segments of one," firms will eventually come up against a disquieting reality: that burrowing ever deeper into data about individual transactions eventually yields only short-term tactical advantage and misses one big and inevitable outcome. When every competitor becomes equally good at predicting each customer's next purchase, all of the companies will spend effort and money to capture that purchase. In fact, they'll spend so much effort and money that they'll wipe out their profits from the marginal transaction. This unwinnable arms race ultimately leads to an equalization of competitors in the medium to long term. There is little lasting advantage from one-to-one targeting. This is not to say firms should never try to predict and capture the next purchase. But they should expect above-average returns from this activity only in industries where competitors are lagging and where there are still some rewards to being ahead of the game. In many industries, including travel, insurance, telecom, and even automobiles, we are rapidly closing in on equalization, so there is little lasting competitive advantage to be gained: the one-to-one playing field is rapidly getting leveled.

Unlike individual customer information and the race to capture the next transaction, the mountains of data now available can be used to construct a big-picture view of customers. The big picture that any company develops, the insights that come from it, and the value it can deliver for your customers will always be unique. None of your competitors have the same combination of customers or customer interactions that you have; nor do they see the industry from the same perspective that you do. Their measures are different because their strategic imperatives are different. The pieces of the puzzle that you assemble will be different from those your competitors pick. Your big picture is impossible for competitors to replicate. In fact, they may have no interest in replicating it—their own big picture will provide them with insights their competitors, including you, don't have.

So rather than pursue the next transaction by developing an ever more detailed picture of the customer, step back to look at the big picture. When the detail of individual-level data is assembled into something meaningful, the big picture can have transformative value. Like Nadar, marketers should consider moving from portrait to aerial photography.

Obstacles to the Big Picture

One of the first hurdles you will encounter in capturing the big picture and extracting value from it is a blind spot. You often do not recognize that what you know (or could know) is of value to your customers. Resolving this blind spot is the first step to seeing the big picture.

In a day-long meeting with the three divisional presidents of a large seller of farm supplies, I learned that over the previous couple of years, the key challenge for the company had been to protect its $4 billion revenue stream from being eroded by increasingly aggressive competitors offering very similar seeds, fertilizers, and pesticides. On the face of it, the company's response was very downstream: to strengthen the front line, train and empower its salespeople, align their incentives, and bolster service to deepen relationships with individual customers. These initiatives were designed to prevent the company's primary customers, retail farm-store owners and farmers, from switching to its competitors. And the strategies had worked for a while. A salesperson in a rural area was held up as an example of best practice. This frontline account representative had won the trust of independent retail store owners by providing unrivaled service and attention to their business, sometimes even holding the store for a few hours while the owner stepped out to run errands. This salesperson had received a companywide sales award, and others had been exhorted to emulate him.

But when this account rep left to join the competition, the company realized that its efforts had made the customers loyal to the frontline salespeople, not to the company. The company had failed to offer its customers a value proposition that would win their lasting loyalty.

Adding service to its increasingly undifferentiated products by strengthening the front line had not kept customers from switching. It was time to examine other strategies.

To break out of the cycle of increasing frontline costs and downward price pressures, the company took a step back to look at the big picture. Drawing on its roots as a cooperative, the company established a team of agronomists to collect and study input and output data from farms across many regions. The team's task was to determine the effect of various inputs and farming practices (e.g., seed varieties, fertilizer and pesticide usage, and irrigation practices) on key output measures such as yield rates and output quality for a large variety of crops and field conditions. Like ICI in the quarry market, the company was able to develop a big-picture understanding of the input-output relationships across a wide variety of conditions. It could build models of the optimal levels of fertilizer, pesticide, and irrigation for different climatic and soil conditions. None of its individual customers had that kind of knowledge, but all the customers were keen to see where they stood in relation to others and to identify gaps in their own practices.

The results of the data analysis were fed back to farmers through the sales reps, who were now equipped to show the customers how their farms compared with others of similar size and characteristics on various input and output dimensions. A tweak in fertilizer or pesticide levels could increase output or reduce costs. Farmers were able to adjust their farming practices in response and indicated that it helped them understand what they were doing right or wrong. The salespeople felt empowered because they were now bringing to their customers unique knowledge and value that their competitors could not. Importantly, the company had built a competitive advantage that resided at the core of the organization, not at the level of the individual salesperson or on the front line. This competitive advantage was secure even when an individual salesperson moved on. And since the system information was constantly updated using data from the field, it remained a powerful differentiator even as competitors attempted to emulate it.

This kind of competitive lead helps the firm focus on customer needs, rather than being chased into product and price decisions by competitors nipping at its heels. Competition appears far less intense, both on the front line and on the bottom line, and buyers are now loyal to the firm, not just to the sales force. Just as importantly, the company is able to attract and keep better frontline people, who appreciate the evidence-based selling environment that the company provides, their own role as advisers, and the value created for the customers.

The Big Picture's Potential

The big picture creates value because it allows you to anticipate problems, learn of potential solutions, and avoid dead ends. In each instance, the two underlying sources of value to customers remain constant: you can help reduce their costs, you can reduce their risks, or you can do both.

Take, for example, the Zagat Survey, or what the *Wall Street Journal* dubs the "gastronomic bible." This family business was started by Nina and Tim Zagat in 1979 as a hobby with a simple premise: that the opinions of thousands of regular restaurant-goers count for more than those of a few professional critics. The founders began conducting an annual survey of consumers on their opinions of where to eat, drink, and sleep around the globe. Over three decades, Zagat has become one of the most trusted sources of restaurant, hotel, and bar rankings and other information for millions of consumers, helping them make informed decisions. The value created by the Zagat rankings is simple. They recognize the importance of accurate information for the consumer in service categories where you can't really gauge quality prior to purchase. You can only tell the quality of a restaurant once you've eaten there—and then it is too late. So Zagat aggregates the experience of 350,000 other consumers and mirrors that information back to its subscribers—so they don't have to incur the costs or the risks of trying an unfamiliar restaurant or spending a sleepless night in a dodgy hotel.

Over time, as consumers come to rely on Zagat, the brand becomes synonymous with a way to reduce costs and risks prior to trying a product or service. The reputation and strength of the Zagat brand have enabled the company to expand its information service into new categories and subcategories relating to food and leisure, such as top live entertainment, romance best bets, and even top golf courses and top shopping places.

The Zagat business model, too, is simple. In addition to selling its books that are designed to fit in a pocket, Zagat is present on the web, where it charges annual membership fees for access to its restaurant ratings online. Inevitably, the company also has a a paid mobile application. Across platforms and consumption categories, the underlying premise remains the same: consumers will pay to reduce risks and costs. And it is partly for this reason that Zagat was acquired by Google in 2011.

The Big Picture as Business Model

In twenty-first-century information businesses, the big picture is rapidly becoming an indispensable tool. Firms are recognizing that a bird's-eye view is a competitive advantage and a source of value to customers. But some businesses go farther—the big picture *is* their business. Like Bluefin Labs, which gauges Twitter reactions to ads, and Zagat, and TripAdvisor, the travel information website, these companies are founded on the insight that aggregating data and reflecting the big picture back to customers is of value to those customers.

INRIX, a Seattle start-up, began with the idea that real-time traffic information is valuable to drivers, fleet owners, road operators, GPS information providers, the media and other resellers, and many other users. INRIX pieced together information from cell-phone towers located near roadways. It collected data about the number of phones that were connected to the tower at any given time. The direction and speed of movement of the cars connected to the towers could be determined as the phones' connections were handed from one cell tower to the next. This information could be combined with road capacity data to assemble a real-time big picture of traffic congestion and patterns. Would customers pay to access this big picture?

Over time, INRIX has added many sources of traffic information, including traditional road sensors and even local event calendars such as concerts, sports games, and conventions, to build a triangulated real-time picture of traffic. Perhaps the most interesting of these other sources of information is the company's version of crowdsourcing, called SmartDriver. Over two million participating drivers use GPS or the INRIX traffic app from the App Store. As they drive, the drivers' apps automatically feed information about traffic speed and conditions back into the central database, where the data is aggregated and analyzed to produce meaningful traffic reports. Users get accurate forecasts of road congestion, actual accident reports, warnings about road works, and so on. Customers pay a subscription to access the big-picture information to which their own phone app contributed a bit or two.

Similarly, CitySense, a mobile phone application by Sense Networks, tells you where the party action is in any given city. This application makes smart use of the user's location information. It provides mash-ups of GPS data from taxis in major US cities with maps from Google Maps and information from Yelp to identify the traffic in individual restaurants, bars, shops, and other points of interest, providing the app users with a heat map of social activities in the city. But it gets better. The application is built to understand what type of user the phone's owner is. It records the behavior of users (locations they visit and when) and aggregates this information with that of other users to form a big picture. From the big picture, the data-crunching behind the app identifies lifestyle segments. These segments are displayed in different colors on the heat map, so the application doesn't answer only the question "Where is everybody hanging out?" but also answers the more critical question "Where is everybody like me hanging out?" This means that users are able to identify restaurants they would like, events they would enjoy, and people they share interests with in any city in which the application is available.

Bluefin Labs, INRIX, and CitySense are examples of a new breed of business—ones built entirely on the value of the big picture. These companies resolve the inherent information asymmetry between individuals and the big picture. An individual cannot predict traffic conditions, but the aggregation of data from thousands of individuals allows INRIX to make such predictions with reasonable accuracy.

These companies stand out as examples of big-picture businesses because they are in the information business. But in the twenty-first century, isn't every business an information business? As we've seen, in the explosives, agricultural inputs, traffic information, and other businesses, big-picture information offers a new form of value.

Perhaps because most firms are so busy pushing product out the door, they neglect to step back, look at the big picture, and appreciate the potential of their own unique perspective. Yet those that do so earn a respite from the ravages of commodity competition and build a sustainable differentiation that fosters customer loyalty. Capitalizing on the value of *your* view of the forest requires setting up systems to collect, aggregate, analyze, and share customer-experience data. Any firm with more than a handful of customers can do this.

Sharing what you see from your privileged perch can be very valuable to your customers and surprisingly rewarding for you. You can gain both customer engagement and market stature by becoming the conduit by which customers learn about the larger context, find solutions, and avoid dead ends. You can gain pricing flexibility because of the added value you bring, and you can gain customer loyalty because customers can't get that added value from your competitors. The big picture is a quintessentially downstream competitive advantage that is based on your perspective on the marketplace. To grasp it requires you to tilt.

In the next chapter, we'll dive into three distinct ways to exploit the information value of the big picture for the benefit of your customers. Specifically, we will look at strategies of relaying and connecting, benchmarking and mirroring, and predicting.

The Big-Picture Checklist

As you consider assembling your own big picture, it is worth keeping in mind the following principles and asking the related questions:

✓ What would your customers like to know? Specifically, what types of information will help them reduce their costs or their risks?

✓ What type of information is currently widely dispersed, but would yield new insight if aggregated? Is there any incidentally produced data (such as keystrokes or location data) that could be valuable when assembled?

✓ Are your customers diverse enough that they will benefit from aggregating their data with others'? (If there is little diversity or variance, there is little benefit for customers because most other customers are exactly like them.)

✓ What are the costs and benefits of assembling the data? Can you spell out the benefits? Can you run a pilot project to reduce your risks?

✓ How will you use the big picture? Will it be a product, an added service for your customers, or simply added insight for you to deliver your products and services better?

✓ Will the big picture change the way you look at your business? Will it change your understanding of your core competences and competitive advantage?

✓ Can you enlist customers to contribute the data? Are you the first ones in the industry to do so?

5. Extracting Value from the Big Picture

Marketing today faces a challenge no less significant than the one that jolted it into the mass era a little over a century ago. Then, factories that had adopted mass production were spewing out inexpensively manufactured products faster than the market could absorb them. The industrialization of agriculture created a glut of farm products. The mechanization and assembly-lining of various industries dropped productions costs of manufactured goods by 90 percent. The bottlenecks in the value chain were no longer in resource scarcity or manufacturing, but lay in demand: in the ability of consumers to understand, make sense of, and buy the products rolling out of the factories. Marketing and, in particular, brands eased the bottlenecks by turning commodity products into packaged consumer value, facilitating the development of mass media, and creating the "brandscapes" that we all live in today. Wrigley's, Coca-Cola, Kellogg, Ford, Heinz, Levi's, Ivory and Sunlight soaps, and Budweiser, to name but a few, became household names because they found a way to use mass media to efficiently convince large numbers of consumers to buy, and thus create mass demand for, mass-produced goods. Savvy manufacturers clued in to brands because they offered a form of micro-monopoly—customers and consumers no longer saw competitive brands as substitutes, but saw each brand as offering a unique value proposition. Brands became a powerful and enduring competitive advantage, a bulwark against competitors. Marketing had dealt with the challenge of mass production with an effective response: mass brands that then went on to change the marketplaces we live in. Today, in the early decades of the twenty-first century, marketing faces a similarly monumental challenge.

The petabytes spewing out from the billions of consumer interactions, transactions, and other events hold the promise of answering questions about everything marketers always wanted to know about their customers, but didn't have the data to ask. Any firm can now link consumers' media habits with their purchase habits. It can track individual customers, gauge their brand and store loyalty, and even assess their influence on other customers. And it can see patterns others have not seen before and strengthen customer relationships by making them deeper, more meaningful, and less transaction-based. What marketers do with the data, and how they convert it into customer value, will determine whether the data provides an enduring competitive advantage or triggers a race to the bottom. In this chapter, we look at three ways in which the marketplace information can create value for your customers: relaying and connecting, benchmarking and mirroring, and predicting. You will recognize some of the cases we've already seen as they find their place as examples of these strategies. Let's start with the most basic, relaying and connecting.

Relaying and Connecting

Relaying and connecting are simple ideas—ones that are intuitively practiced by many businesses on an ad hoc basis. You take information from one location and apply it in another. You learn from one customer and use that learning to help another. You act as a connector between two parties that can benefit from knowing each other. If you'd like an analogy, think of your company as a satellite with a large footprint. You can take information from one location and relay it to other parts of the world, creating value for the receiver and perhaps also for yourself, the sender. You can connect a buyer and seller. Despite the simplicity of these ideas, it takes considerable skill and organizational ability to implement this type of information arbitrage systematically. Large and dispersed organizations with wide footprints tend to be the best-placed groups to implement this idea because of their span across different geographical areas, industries, or markets. But there is nothing to prevent any business with more than one customer or supplier from creating value through relaying and connecting.

As with all three big-picture information strategies, your advantage is that you have a view of the forest where your customers can only see the trees. Your company, from its perch over all of its customers, sees ideas and solutions that have been implemented or tried. You know those that worked and those that did not. Many of those solutions could be very valuable to other customers in other locations, industries, or contexts. Yet those customers often have no means of accessing the knowledge that you take for granted, thanks to your view of the entire playing field.

Consider Hilti, a privately held Liechtenstein-based maker of high-end power tools and fastening systems. The company's information-relaying network accounts for its strong competitive advantage in its industry. Virtually all of Hilti's nearly $5 billion in sales are made to professional builders, contractors, and construction companies. Although several of these customers are larger than Hilti, many aren't very international—in fact, there are few global players in the construction industry anywhere. Most firms in the industry remain confined within national boundaries because of, among other things, national building codes, local needs and building practices, and local sourcing of materials and labor. But the lack of global players does not mean that the problems faced during construction are all that different at various locations. Complex problems, those having to do with the realization of complex architectural designs or resulting from the choice of new or exotic materials, are familiar to builders in many parts of the world. Solutions to these problems are familiar to Hilti, because the company has seen them solved elsewhere in its network. This is the relaying opportunity on which Hilti builds its competitive advantage.

With a presence in over 120 countries worldwide, Hilti fills the geographic information gap for customers who would like to know what is happening elsewhere in the world. These customers value the information that Hilti can bring them, but they don't have the time, the resources, or the span and vision to gather it on their own. A cornerstone of Hilti's relaying capability is its direct sales system. Through this system, more than thirteen thousand of its twenty-two thousand employees work and exchange information. Over a hundred thousand customer contacts are logged each day, including information about the kinds of products customers are buying, the kinds of problems they are facing, and the solutions Hilti is suggesting. To complement this networking capability, Hilti has purposely defined its business processes uniformly around the world. This uniform approach enables individual sales representatives and customer support engineers to routinely access solutions developed in another part of the network to support local customers.

One Hilti customer, a Brunei-based operator of over two hundred offshore oil and gas production platforms, faced a problem that was unrelated to its core business, but was nevertheless a persistent nuisance and safety hazard. The walkways on its ocean-based platforms required continual repair and renovation because of the effects of corrosion and severe weather. Of particular concern were the walkways and gratings in the wave zone—the parts of the structure that were washed over by powerful waves. Hilti is not in the business of selling walkways or gratings. Still, once Hilti learned of the problem, its global information network kicked into action. A North American supplier of fiberglass walkways had earlier approached Hilti to find a way to fasten these walkways to construction platforms. Fiberglass was a natural solution to the problems of corrosion and excess wear and tear, but had not been extensively tried. Data on Hilti's fastening experience from Europe's North Sea platforms was combined with information about the new material, while the Singapore office conducted pilot tests to adapt the solution to local conditions. The result for the customer was a customized walkway solution that was assembled from pieces of information in Hilti's network around the world.

Few other companies could have matched this kind of rapid information integration from distributed global locations. Hilti benefited in two ways. It supplied the system that fastened the gratings to the platform, and it acquired a satisfied customer. Hilti and its customers consider the company's customer orientation, application know-how, and advisory skills important company strengths that justify its premium prices in an otherwise competitive marketplace. Indeed, many Hilti employees refer to the company as an information network that happens to sell power tools and fastening systems.

On the face of it, relaying information is a relatively straightforward process. And on an ad hoc basis, it is: bringing information to a customer about what happened elsewhere seems simple enough. But as the Hilti example illustrates, successful relaying is more than that. Turning relaying into a competitive advantage requires more than a onetime transfer of information from one location to another. Customers will only reward suppliers for their perspective if the supplier can be relied upon to consistently bring innovative and relevant solutions to thorny problems. They are looking for reliable relaying capabilities, not just instances of relaying. This requires the supplier to build the systems to collect and collate information from a vast global network, and to turn that knowledge into viable customer solutions. The relaying function has to be institutionalized, rather than left to the initiative of enterprising and empowered frontline people. Not surprisingly, these types of information systems are the most developed in information-intensive online businesses that have very large numbers of customers. Amazon .com's systems stand out.

Value through Relaying and Connecting

Amazon.com has grown from zero to more than $65 billion in annual sales in a a decade and a half. During that time, the company has revolutionized retailing, emerging as a challenger to the world's largest general merchandisers, including Walmart. As part of a strategy of consolidation into a vast online mall, the retailer has acquired several dedicated retail category leaders in the online shopping space, including Zappos in shoes and Diapers.com in baby products. So how did a bookstore grow big enough to buy the other category-focused retailers? Why didn't an online general merchandise retailer come out of, say, the general merchandise business? And how is it that in an "experience economy," Amazon.com was able to neutralize challenges from brick-and-mortar booksellers that offered not just books, but also hot coffee, comfortable leather reading chairs, meet-the-author events, immediate product delivery, and cozy reading club meetings?

The answer is that customers get much more than books at Amazon .com, too—and a large part of that additional value resides in *relayed* experience and *connections* with other readers and consumers who provide valuable information. Not only does Amazon.com allow the customer to shop online at any time he or she chooses, in any time zone, but the customer also gets extensive information and advice unavailable in a traditional store. A book customer can see the book cover, read its first chapter, browse its table of contents, flip through the jacket, and peek at the Amazon.com best-seller lists to see what others are reading, all in the comfort of their pajamas in the middle of the night, from anywhere on the planet. But the kicker is that the customer can also browse through what other readers think of the book—their detailed reviews are available twenty-four hours a day and are sortable and searchable. Furthermore, at the click of a mouse, the reader can find out about other books that have been bought by buyers of the book being considered—if the customer has just finished reading a book he or she enjoyed, this is a great way to find other books of the same type—books the customer might not otherwise have heard of or considered. Amazon.com builds on the idea of the best-seller list and individualizes it. As with the City-Sense app we encountered earlier, you don't just learn what others are reading; you get the answer to a more personalized question: "What are others *like me* reading?" And if you are a repeat customer, Amazon.com provides you with highly accurate and targeted recommendations of books, DVDs, and the like—merchandise that is bound to be of interest because your purchase and browsing history has been matched against the company's database of more than 150 million customers.

Platforms for Relaying and Connecting

At its core, the big picture is an advantage of perspective—your location in the marketplace gives you a view that others do not have. In relaying, you translate the big-picture perspective into competitive advantage by aggregating, analyzing, and retransmitting the information to customers. Through this mechanism, your company occupies the central node in a network that radiates from it—all information flows first to and then from this central node. But a more radical possibility exists: connecting different parts of the network that would not otherwise connect. By doing this, your firm becomes a critical, indispensable node. Amazon.com connects readers (and consumers) by offering them a forum to share product and consumption experiences. This connection creates value and more sales for the company. But Amazon.com also connects thousands of small store owners, who can set up storefronts within Amazon.com's digital mall and gain access to consumers who visit the Amazon.com site. The store owners and consumers might never otherwise have connected. The consumer feels comfortable buying from these smaller stores because they are on Amazon.com, and the smaller stores pay Amazon.com for access to its two hundred million consumers and to a common platform of search, billing, and payment services. Similar connecting strategies are evident in the iTunes store, where content owners are connected to content consumers, and in the various app stores that connect application developers with users.

While most upstream businesses think in terms of selling more (moving more stuff through an existing infrastructure), connecting is the result of asking what else customers want. The result can be as ambitious as creating new market spaces and building and owning the platforms on which others trade the stuff that customers want.

One strategic challenge in connecting is determining the degree of control over the platform. Clearly, the company needs to have enough control to maintain standards and quality and to capture a share of the value the platform has created. Apple's platforms tend to be tightly controlled and give the company a greater share of the revenues. The company uses the control to maintain high levels of quality. But the company's tight control over its platforms is also its Achilles' heel in the face of competition from more open platforms created by competitors. iTunes is a great platform for searching, storing, organizing, and listening to digital content. But it turned its back on content *sharing,* perhaps because it was designed as a counterpoint to the illegal music sharing on sites such as Napster, Gnutella, Kazaa, and LimeWire. Now, the biggest competitive challenge for iTunes comes from companies that create social platforms for the legal sharing of music, such as Spotify, with its seamless integration into Facebook, and Google Music with its integration into Google's many services.

A closed, tightly controlled platform is also an invitation to competitors to launch one that is more open. Google's Android operating system is a freely licensed operating system that poses a challenge to Apple's operating system. Thousands of phone and tablet hardware manufacturers build Android into their gadgets. With multiple hardware companies selling Android gadgets, the operating system gains on market presence—which is a key success metric in technology markets, where interoperability of gadgets is important. Worldwide, the Android platform has rapidly reached an 80 percent market share on smartphones. On the downside, the Android system's market presence is more chaotic than that of Apple's operating system in that many versions of the platform exist simultaneously in the marketplace. Some are older versions that have not been updated by Google; other versions have been customized or adapted by licensees such as Samsung, LG, HTC, and other phone manufacturers. Upgrade cycles are not synchronized across manufacturers or telecom carriers, so some of the advantages of market heft are lost in the chaos of multiple versions. Control of open platforms remains a challenge, even for large and technologically savvy companies like Google.

Several other rivals have identified that the vulnerability in fortress Apple is indeed its tightly controlled, closed connecting platforms.

Nuance Communications, a company that makes voice recognition software, has developed an open system alternative to Apple's artificial intelligence assistant, Siri.[1] Unlike Siri, Nuance's system, Nina, can be used by third-party developers. They can integrate the Nina software into apps such as banking and smartphone security, and other customized apps. Apple's Siri remains a closed platform that is not accessible to third-party developers.

Competitive Advantage

The relaying and connecting functions are not easy for competitors to replicate. Once these functions attract a critical mass of users, they become almost insurmountable barriers to entry. If Amazon.com's competitors wanted to deliver similar information to customers, with similar accuracy and reliability, they would have to replicate the online retailer's vast footprint—its experience with hundreds of millions of customers, and the experience of millions of those customers with each other. Amazon.com's competitive advantage resides, literally, with its customers.

As consumers, we all know that Amazon.com's informational features are designed to get us to buy or buy more. Amazon.com, like any other retailer, wants to maximize the shopping dollars we spend once we are in the store. And by most accounts, this is working rather well—revenues were just over $10 billion in 2006 and have risen fourfold since, during the deepest recession in the United States since the Great Depression. What's more, customers are happy too: the company has consistently been one of the top two online retailers in ForeSee's annual retail satisfaction index since 2005. The other frontrunner is Netflix, whose powerful recommendation engine, like Amazon.com's, remains a long-term competitive advantage.

At the heart of Amazon.com's recommendation engine is the goal of answering a very simple question for customers: "What's going on elsewhere?" The relaying of experience is valuable to all users because no single customer knows what is happening everywhere else in the forest. But Amazon.com's relaying and connecting systems help each customer find the information and products that are relevant to improving his or her experience. This unique added value is as applicable to shoes and baby products, to furniture and electronics, as it is to books. Amazon.com has diversified and acquired other category-focused retailers. While its competitors such as general merchandisers brought to their online operations the mind-set of the offline world: to sell more of the stuff they were already selling, Amazon.com's approach was building information channels to relay information. And just as in the ICI mining example we saw in chapter 4, this type of competitive advantage has a unique characteristic: the more customers Amazon.com gains, the more informative its reviews become, the more accurate its recommendations are, the more value it adds to customers, and the more business it does at a lower cost. And the less likely it is that competitors can replicate these advantages—its barriers to entry escalate with a larger installed base of customers.

Relaying and connecting are the most valuable when physical or perceptual barriers such as distance, industry boundaries, or knowledge and information fences prevent customers from learning from each other or from accessing other parts of the market. The seller can help bridge the information gap. Where customers find it difficult or costly to learn about new developments or ideas that might be relevant to their own situation, the seller brings efficient access to knowledge and solutions developed elsewhere. Customers find this valuable because it spares them the time, effort, and energy required to reinvent the wheel—especially in areas that are not core to their business or their lives. The common underlying feature of the relaying and connecting strategies is that they reduce customers' cost of search, evaluation, comparison, and decision making and reduce the customers' risks of choosing the wrong product.

Benchmarking and Mirroring

Benchmarking provides customers with the all-important "you are here" location on dimensions that are relevant to them. This information allows them to pinpoint their own position relative to their peers on crucial metrics. Decisions and behavior can change as a result of this knowledge. Households, for example, reduce their energy consumption more and recycle more if they can compare themselves to other known households, such as those of their neighbors or friends, than if they are only given their own consumption data over time.[2] Opower, a utility billing company, allows users to plug in and compare their electricity bills with their Facebook friends. The result: significant drops in electricity consumption for those who do.

Benchmarking is a special case of a more general use of the big picture: mirroring. Mirroring, or reflecting the big-picture view back to individual customers, is probably the most common application of the big picture. Think back to the examples we have already seen: the book best-seller list, Zagat's compilation of crowd-sourced restaurant and hotel reviews, INRIX's traffic patterns, and CitySense's heat maps indicating social activity. Each example aggregates and feeds back to individuals information about groups of customers. Having seen several examples of mirroring in the previous chapter, in this section we will concentrate on benchmarking.

The value and availability of benchmarking data has increased with the growth of the third-party benchmarking industry, as well as in social comparisons on social networking sites such as Facebook and LinkedIn.[3] Nike+ allows runners to measure running performance and upload their running data to Facebook. Benchmarking against other runners and their own past performance motivates Nike's customers to maintain a training regimen. But benchmarking existed well before social media sites.

Well-known examples of benchmarking by third parties include the J.D. Power and Associates car-quality evaluations, which motivate car companies to pay attention to certain dimensions of quality; *Fortune* magazine's World's Most Admired Companies list, which publicly ranks companies that other companies admire; and the Socrates Index of Corporate Social Responsibility. These types of third-party rankings by data aggregators that are in the business of benchmarking have the advantage of being perceived as impartial. But seller-conducted benchmarks can be even more valuable because suppliers often have access to data that third parties can't get their hands on. For example, a supplier of office automation equipment knows much more about the document-handling practices of buying organizations than does an office automation industry association or a third-party research company. The seller can provide buyers with benchmark data on paper consumption and on copying and printing intensity during the day, the week, and the year, so that buyers can modify their workflow practices and paper and toner inventory, if needed.

Benchmarking by suppliers helps customers answer questions such as these: Is my productivity above or below the industry standard? Am I spending more or less than others on information technology? Are my practices as environmentally sound as those of others? Are my servers operating above or below average speed? Do I get more or fewer page-views and click-throughs on my website and advertisements? Is my electricity consumption above or below that of my neighbors? Are my workout runs longer or more intensive? Customers crave this kind of information because it helps them better understand the environment in which they operate, and it allows them to alter their own behavior.

Much has been written about benchmarking, most of it in the form of consulting or DIY guides aimed at managers who want to find out how their company stacks up against competitors and peers. The volume of the literature reveals a great demand for benchmarking information. But the neglected opportunity in benchmarking is for suppliers, which have a big picture of the industry, to help customers benchmark on variables that are of interest to both.

How Benchmarking Changed an Industry

A small and fragmented, yet global and interesting little industry has been dramatically altered over the past two decades because a third-party benchmarked the players on certain dimensions of quality. The industry was not benchmarked by a supplier, yet it carries significant lessons for suppliers because the benchmarking exercise had such far-reaching effects. It reconfigured, forever, the allocation of resources by each of the players. The benchmarking occurred in the business school industry. It started with *BusinessWeek*'s rankings of MBA programs in 1988, and its effects continue to be felt a quarter century later.

Prior to 1988, business schools competed more for faculty than they did for students. Reputation has always been an important criterion for both faculty and students in their choice of business school. But a school's reputation, a fuzzy concept that means different things to different people, is not necessarily based on hard or recent data. In fact, reputations tend to be based on hard-to-measure things such as the school's history, the halo of the university's reputation on its business school, and the performance of highly visible alumni. But are these the relevant criteria for a prospective student choosing a school?

Media publications such as *BusinessWeek* and, later, the *Financial Times* asked this question and concluded that they could define more relevant measures of business school quality. These publications began ranking business schools on "objective" criteria, including surveys of alumni, the dollar value of salary jumps from admission to graduation as well as three years after graduation, the diversity of the student body and faculty (proportion of women, proportion of international students and faculty), recruiter feedback, the quantity and impact of faculty research, the student's return on investment on the cost of the program, and so on.

The initial purpose of the rankings was to provide a guide for students considering MBA programs. Or, more strategically for the media outlets publishing the lists, the purpose was to attract new readers and sell more copies by publishing information that was relevant to the choices of critical segments. Large numbers of MBA applicants, alumni, recruiters, and donors are interested in school standings in the rankings. In fact, the Bloomberg *BusinessWeek* MBA rankings issue is the largest-selling issue of the year, the business equivalent of *Sports Illustrated*'s swimsuit issue. The publications knew they had hit pay dirt when advertisers looking to target MBA applicants began to buy ad space, reinforcing the publications' motivation for conducting the rankings. The business schools themselves were, of course, among those lining up to buy ad space. But within a few years, things got really interesting: the impact the rankings had on the industry extended far beyond serving as an informational input to the decisions of MBA aspirants, far beyond selling a few thousand more copies of magazines.

Through the 1990s and the first decade of this century, the globalization of the student pool has changed the nature of business school admissions. Globalization has brought much more intense competition among business schools for the best candidates, who are now much more mobile and willing to move, often to a different country, to get the best education. Lacking direct information and local knowledge, candidates from far-flung places often seek independent information and quality validation about possible schools and their MBA programs. This need coincided with the rise of the rankings.

As candidates' criteria for choosing a business school became increasingly driven by the rankings, schools found themselves competing on dimensions that had earlier barely made a blip on their strategic radars. Suddenly, they were scrambling to set up career-management departments to improve relations with high-paying recruiters, they were vying to recruit more women and international students and faculty, and they were nudging their faculty to publish in academic journals monitored by the rankings list. The schools bolstered their outreach to alumni, especially people who had graduated up to three years earlier, to reinforce this group's positive memories of the school. Some business schools were even selecting students on the basis of the individuals' ability to get high-paying finance and consulting jobs upon graduation so that the graduates could show a salary bump and a high return on the MBA investment, both criteria used by the rankings.[4]

There was a lot at stake. Schools soon found that if they did well in the rankings, they attracted many more applicants, and if they dropped in the rankings, the applicant pool dried up very quickly. Schools that had large applicant pools were able to significantly increase both the quality of their students and their program fees. While university education in general has become much more expensive in recent years,

MBA programs were among the first and most aggressive fee-raisers. One study found that the fee premium charged by schools in the top 10 percent of the *Financial Times* rankings versus those in the bottom 10 percent was about 100 percent.

In sum, the rankings radically altered the behavior of business schools and helped determine their success or decline over the past two decades. The ratings influenced the schools' resource allocation and strategy, their student admission and faculty recruitment, and their pricing ability. Not surprisingly, the most radical structural changes occurred along the dimensions that made up the rankings. Other parts of university campuses that were not subject to such rankings were left wondering what all the commotion was about over at the business school.

Applying Benchmarking to Your Industry

Now think about your industry and your customers. Can you claim any such degree of influence over your customers' behavior? Do your customers alter their resource allocation, their long-term choices, and other decisions because of any information that you provide? If not, benchmarking may be your lever. It has the power to radically alter the agenda and behavior of entire industries and entire customer segments. What gets measured really does get managed.[5] Companies are increasingly measuring and reporting benchmarks on key variables for their customers. Banks that sell corporate treasury management services, for example, offer their customers benchmarks for working capital efficiency to let them know where they stand in relation to peers. Software companies are benchmarking usage and productivity. And as we saw earlier, utilities are not just benchmarking—they are allowing their customers to benchmark their usage against peer groups of their choice (e.g., Facebook friends and neighborhood averages). What's more, measurement companies such as J.D. Power and Associates (customer satisfaction and quality measurements) and Comscore (Internet analytics) are constantly issuing valuable benchmark data for industries to attract clients to their information and consulting services.

Predicting

The most sophisticated use of marketplace data lies in discerning patterns that can help predict future trends. In the previous chapter, we looked at several examples of predicting. ICI's use of blast data to predict the outcomes of explosions allowed the company to create value for quarries by reducing their costs and risks of explosions. The agricultural inputs company used its empirical models to predict farm output on the basis of levels of seed, fertilizer, and pesticide inputs. An analysis of tweets on the social medium Twitter predicted stock market movements and a new movie's box office take. And INRIX can predict, using its models of traffic flow, where traffic snarls will occur. In each of these cases, the data used to make predictions already existed, but was unused by the customer. These companies recognized the data as an asset and were able to assemble it, wring it through predictive models, and generate insights that otherwise would have remained unavailable.

When Google was founded, little did the founders know that they might one day be able to tell, a few weeks before you could, whether the flu was coming to your town. Today the company knows this because over the years, it has developed a big-picture view of Internet users—which by now includes almost everybody. From its vantage point atop the Internet, Google can discern patterns in the web where most others can see only the strands. And it is using this view for interesting applications.

One such application is the prediction of where influenza—the flu—will strike next. Each year, the flu strikes between 5 percent and 20 percent of the population in the United States; more than 200,000 people are hospitalized due to flu complications, and about 36,000 people die. Extrapolation to global populations indicates that at least 500,000 deaths are attributable to the flu each year. An overwhelming majority of these occur among vulnerable populations such as older people, young children, and people with preexisting health conditions. The costs to the economy are nothing to sneeze at, either: the annual bill is estimated at over $100 billion in the United States alone.

A rapidly spreading worldwide flu-like epidemic is considered one of the greatest dangers facing humanity. The pandemic of 1918 claimed between 20 million and 40 million lives. With these daunting statistics, it is not surprising that doctors and researchers know a lot about influenza viruses and health authorities expend considerable effort tracking and preventing outbreaks. They know *when* influenza will strike (*flu season* is part of our lexicon). They know *what* strain of the influenza will strike in a given year, and they design vaccines to combat the predicted genetic variant. They know *how* the disease progresses and *who* will likely develop complications. However, they do not know *where* flu outbreaks will occur. The current procedures used—collecting, tabulating, and disseminating data on influenza-like illness from visits to emergency rooms and sentinel physicians—result in a one- to two-week delay, limiting the data's predictive value.

This time lag is significant. The population does not know that it may be at heightened risk, health-care providers cannot incorporate base-rate information in their diagnoses, and public health officials may miss the opportunity to develop appropriate health campaigns. The supply-chain effects of an early warning would be even more pronounced. Hospitals, clinics, and doctors' offices could stock up on flu tests, antiviral drugs, and antibiotics for people who get what are known as co-infections, bacterial infections that worsen a bout of flu. Knowing sooner where the flu will strike could save lives.

This is where Google Flu Trends (www.google.org/flutrends) comes in. Every day, hundreds of millions of people turn to Google for searches on every conceivable topic. Because a search is very purposeful, Google works on the reasonable assumption that what is typed in the search bar is an accurate representation of intentions. Extracting meaning across millions of searches yields insights that are unavailable to individuals. This big picture can have significant value. And Google Flu Trends extracts that value by aggregating the searches and plotting the data over geographical locations (and, conceivably, other variables).

Google reasoned that when people feel ill, they tend to turn to the Internet for information before heading off to the doctor. By tracking searches for things like "flu symptoms" or "muscle aches" by region and state over time, the analysts sought to relate specific search terms with future spikes in the Centers for Disease Control (CDC) influenza-like illness data. Looking back over five years of patterns, Google Flu Trends was able to develop a predictive system that correlated well with the CDC numbers. And as the Internet allows for real-time compilation of the data, Google Flu Trends can provide indications of regional influenza outbreaks seven to ten days earlier than the CDC's current process. The model continues to be refined as search behavior changes. For example, in the 2012–2013 flu season in the United States, Flu Trends overestimated its flu predictions because of a feedback effect: more people were searching for flu-related terms on Google because there was more media coverage of the flu and more social media discussion of the flu. But calibration issues are inherent to any measurement technology in its infancy. The predictive model will become more accurate with more data.

Consider that the value of Google Flu Trends is entirely the result of seeing a picture that others cannot or did not see and from recognizing and using an asset that so often remains dormant and overlooked by companies: their own big picture of their customers. And every company, in every industry, has one.

The ability to predict outcomes is one of the most sophisticated uses of the big picture and one of the most valuable. Prediction requires advanced analytic skills and creates unique differentiation. The data on which predictions are made is often either proprietary or difficult to assemble into a big picture, and the skills required to process the data are uncommon. For this reason, the company that does go to the trouble of building predictive skills earns a competitive advantage that is difficult to replicate.

Relaying and connecting, benchmarking and mirroring, and predicting are three mechanisms for extracting customer value from the big picture. With each technique, you use your location—your perch, or your view of the entire downstream playing field—to develop insights about your customers' needs, wants, and challenges. Insights from each of the mechanisms discussed in this chapter help reduce customers' costs and risks. In other words, the reduction of those costs and risks becomes a part of your downstream innovation efforts—part of your tilt.

The Big-Picture Checklist

In light of our earlier (chapter 2) analysis of costs and risks at each customer interaction point, it is now worth asking several questions:

- ✓ What are the information asymmetries in the markets that you serve? What do you know about your customers that they don't? What do some of them not know that others do? Where do your customers have knowledge that could be useful elsewhere?
- ✓ What types of information would help reduce customers' costs and risks?
- ✓ Where does the information reside?
- ✓ What systems, behaviors, and procedures do you need to collect and store the information on a regular basis?
- ✓ What kinds of insights will help your customers reduce their costs and risks? What types of models, aggregation techniques, and visualization tools will help you build a useful big picture?
- ✓ How do you deploy the information back to customers? Should you sell or give away the insights from the big picture? Should the big picture be a stand-alone product or business line?
- ✓ How does deploying the information create competitive advantage for you? Are your insights unique? In view of the big picture, what can you say that others cannot?
- ✓ Is the competitive advantage from your big picture sustainable? If yes, what makes it so?

- ✓ How does exploiting the big picture change the nature of your business? Is the big picture a central part of the value customers expect from you?
- ✓ How does relying on the big picture as a source of competitive advantage change your organization?

Part Three

The Deep Dive

The Competitive Playing Field Inside the Customer's Mind

6. Scoping Out the Playing Field

FedEx encapsulates its value proposition in the tagline "Relax, it's FedEx" or, more recently, "The World on Time." Tide laundry detergent "washes whitest" and has more recently been the "clean you can trust," and Volvo is closely associated in consumers' minds with safety. Any brand is a classic downstream competitive advantage because it is a platform for transactions between the buyer and the seller, it resides in the marketplace, and it reduces customers' costs and risks. With a successful brand in place, the seller has a clear value proposition that both appeals to customers and is distinct from the value propositions of competitors. It is no accident that the brands' positioning and their tag lines are intended to communicate cost or risk reduction.

Brands are ubiquitous in twenty-first-century marketplaces because the costs of building brands—the costs of communicating and consistently delivering on a promise—are lower than the benefits of a clear value proposition in a crowded market. Brands help find and attract customers, and with brands, customers find it easier to locate the products they want and need. Brands make markets more efficient in the sense that buyers and sellers are brought together at lower cost to both parties than would be possible without brands.

The Brand Promise

In a world of practically infinite choice, consumers gravitate toward a brand or product they trust to deliver on its promises. So, to serve as a platform for customers and sellers to come together, your brand builds trust through consistent quality and consistent positioning, over time and over purchase occasions. The brand offers an implicit guarantee that the customers' present and future experiences with the product or service will be similar to their experience with past purchases. Sometimes, customers are willing to pay a premium for the "what you see is what you get" clarity of a brand, and sometimes they simply repeatedly return to their preferred brand because of what marketers term brand loyalty. In either case, the brand reaps a return on the investments it makes to ensure quality and consistency, and these returns act as an incentive to the seller to maintain those investments.

A classic thought experiment in the world of branding is to ask what would happen to Coca-Cola's ability to raise financing and restart operations if all of its physical assets around the world were to mysteriously go up in flames one night. The answer, most reasonable businesspeople conclude, is that the setback would cost the company time, effort, and money, but that Coca-Cola would have little difficulty finding the funds to get back on its feet. Its brand would help the company survive such a crisis and attract investors looking for future returns.

The second part of the thought experiment involves asking what would happen if instead of the loss of the physical assets, seven billion consumers around the world were to wake up one morning with partial amnesia, such that they could not remember the brand name Coca-Cola or any of its associations. In this latter scenario, despite Coca-Cola's physical assets remaining intact, most reasonable businesspeople agree that the company would find it difficult to scare up the funds to start operations again. The loss of the downstream asset, the brand, it turns out, is a more severe blow to the company's ability to continue business than the loss of upstream assets. But hold on, you say. What about Coca-Cola's secret formula? Isn't that a counterexample? The formula is an upstream asset, a proprietary product formulation, without which the company would not be as successful as it is.

The fact, however, is that the secret formula is not so secret and has not been for at least two decades. In 1993, Mark Pendergrast wrote *For God, Country, and Coca-Cola,* a biography of The Coca-Cola Company.[1] In an appendix of the book, he published the formula that he had found in the company's archives while researching the book. If the "sacred formula," as he calls it, has been the secret behind Coca-Cola's success, its publication and availability to competitors should have sent Coca-Cola's share price plunging. It didn't. But partial amnesia among the world's consumers about the brand undoubtedly would.

Vying for the Mind of the Customer

So how do businesses manage their brands? Who within the organization is charged with building and maintaining this all-important downstream source of competitive advantage? In their efforts to build brands and compete for customers, businesses routinely vie for web clicks, page ranks, media visibility, celebrity endorsements, distribution contracts, shelf space, and paid advertising space. They engage in belabored "conversations" with customers on social media sites and track customer behavior using loyalty programs and click-streams. Annual global spending on paid advertising exceeds $500 billion and is growing at about 10 percent per year. Retailers play with store layout, shelf placement, planograms, and shelf-talkers to provide higher-margin brands with greater in-store visibility. They monetize their shop floors by charging manufacturers for placing their products at eye-level and in end-of-aisle displays. Those who manage brands—marketing and brand managers, market research firms, advertising and media agencies, packaging designers, and salespeople—are expert buyers. Marketing and brand managers are expert buyers of these marketplace resources, including media, clicks, and shelf-facing. Their job, as they often see it, is to get more and better resources for their brands at a cheaper price and to put them to more efficient use than their competitors do.

But that is akin to asking Michelangelo what he does and getting the response "I use a chisel." Though an accurate answer, it omits the all-important end-purpose of those actions. Similarly missing from the brand manager's job description is a picture of the battlefield on which the manager plays and the desired result of the brand battle. The playing field may be invisible, but is immensely important: the mind of the consumer. So what exactly are brand managers competing for? How do their efforts contribute to managing the brand? Stepping back from the immediate tactical concerns of efficiency (a cheaper media buy, the development of an effective ad execution, better shelf placement, or search engine optimization), it is worth asking, efficiency for what end? What is the goal? *Tilt*'s answer to this question: the strategic advantage that marketing is ultimately trying to capture is a piece of the customers' mind.

Owning a piece of the customer's mind is a prized downstream competitive advantage. Strategists and marketers in companies often point to their brands as being among their companies' most important assets. As proof, they forward to their skeptical finance colleagues the annual Interbrand global brand rankings, which show that the top twenty brands in the world are together valued at over $800 billion and that the paragon of brands, Coca-Cola, is alone worth over $75 billion.[2] They do so in the hope that perhaps attaching an independently adjudicated tangible dollar value to brands will make it easier to maintain or boost their own marketing budgets or, at the very least, will help convince the hard-nosed CFO and the executive committee that some of the company's marketing expenditures are not wasted. In this line of reasoning, the brand is construed as the end goal of marketing efforts, and attaching a financial value to that goal makes it easier to justify the financial investments required to attain it. While it is useful to keep the financial value of brand investments and returns in mind, the managerial focus on the financial end goal may obscure the process, strategy, game, and tactics and may even detract from effective brand building. The customer's mind—where the brand resides and the game is played—remains somewhat of an enigma to managers.

In a nutshell, the customers' mind is the sum of the customer's attention, the memory capacity they devote to your brand, and what the brand means to them—the associational hooks it has developed in their minds. The time and cognitive effort your customers spend processing information about your brand deserves close management scrutiny. That's the playing field on which your brand competes. This playing field, like any other, has boundaries and rules. A good understanding of how the game is played allows you to build competitive advantage on this mental playing field.

The Boundary of the Playing Field

Let's begin by defining the outside boundary of the playing field. The consumer's mind is a finite resource. The constraints of this finite resource are up against almost infinite marketplace information. No consumer's mind can absorb, interpret, store, recall, and use all of the information in the marketplace or even just the relevant bits. This imbalance between available information and available mental processing and storage capacity gives rise to a necessary principle of scarcity. Without it, there would be no need for firms to compete for awareness and privileged positions in the consumers' mind.

A direct corollary of this principle is the principle of cognitive economy. Cognitive economy states that because their information-processing capacity is finite, customers will often trade off accuracy of results and optimal outcomes for efficiency of information storage and processing.[3] In other words, customers may end up choosing products that are easier to purchase rather than ones that are the best for their purposes, simply because they can't remember everything about products or they don't want to have to think too much about the products (because they'd rather be thinking about other things). This basic principle has many implications, including the mental shortcuts and mental organizing frameworks that consumers use to make sense of the marketplace. We will explore these implications in depth in the next two chapters. But for now, it is useful to note that the principle of cognitive economy underscores that how consumers buy and consume is more important than what they buy and consume. It emphasizes the importance of downstream activities, and underscores the importance of a tilt.

Take, for example, how customers respond to radical innovation. Novel products have very high failure rates. Most of them, whether launched in the grocery store, the technology domain, or business-to-business arena, end up in the discard pile within a year of launch.[4] Yet companies persist in developing and launching radical innovations despite their high failure rates because novel products that do succeed tend to be much more profitable than humdrum innovations. But it turns out that a novel product often fails not because of technological shortcomings, but because customers simply don't know what to make of it—they see too much risk in adopting it or they can't see where this new product would fit in their lives.

When customers do come across a new product, their cognitively economical approach is to try to classify it, to sort it into a familiar bin or category so that they can make sense of it in terms that are already familiar. If they can do this, they can apply knowledge they already have about other instances of the same thing, and that efficiency is valuable when an individual is operating under cognitive economy. For example, coming across a bean bag for the first time, a customer might be confused. But classifying it as a chair clarifies its purpose and usage. This classification, or categorization, is one type of mental organizing framework that consumers use to make sense of the world around them, including the marketplaces in which they work, live, and play.

Early in the life cycle of digital photography, when film-based photography still dominated, Lexar introduced memory cards for digital cameras in a way that bridged the distance between what film photographers were accustomed to and the new product. The memory cards were sold in gold packaging similar to Kodak film, given a speed rating similar to traditional film's light sensitivity ISO rating, and even labeled "digital film." In stores, they were placed alongside photographic film.[5] How the innovation was presented to consumers made it easier for them to understand and compare the product during the transition from traditional film. Later in the book, we look at the strategic implications of a defining feature of the playing field inside the customer's mind: their criteria of purchase.

An understanding of the layout and rules of the competitive playing field is an essential step in the tilt downstream.

The Customer Mind Checklist

- ✓ What do your brand managers manage? Are they more concerned about the physical marketplace than the playing field in the customers' minds? What is the goal of brand management in your organization?
- ✓ How good is your understanding of the playing field inside the customers' mind? What metaphors and vocabulary does your organization use to talk about the playing field?
- ✓ How does your company compete for a piece of the customers' mind? What do you do to increase or improve your share of mind?

7. Taking Control of Criteria of Purchase

If the finite nature of the customer's cognitive capacity defines the outer boundary of the playing field on which brands compete, then the customers' criteria for making a purchase are the inside lines. Cars may be rated on criteria such as performance, safety, sportiness, fuel efficiency, reliability, and environmental friendliness; running shoes on appearance, ability to improve performance, and arch support; medications on efficacy, speed, convenience, and absence of side effects; luggage on strength, weight, and durability; and computers on speed, memory, user-friendliness, and design. Nike, Tide, and Pampers are ranked high on performance, Volvo on safety, the Toyota Prius on environmental friendliness, and computer brands on whether they're armed with Intel chips. Buyers use these criteria not just to decide whether to purchase a brand, but also to organize and make sense of the brands and the marketplace. Whether you know it or not, and whether you like it or not, on the playing field, your brand is positioned along criteria that customers consider important.

Because they are a fundamental organizing frame for customers, criteria are also the basis on which you segment markets, target and position your brands, and develop strategic market positions as sources of competitive advantage. The brand manager's aim is to consolidate the position of the brand on customers' key criteria for making a purchase. But the strategic objective for the brand owners is, or should be, more ambitious: to influence which criteria customers use to make sense of the market environment and to evaluate and choose among brands in the product category. The marketer's goal is to alter the relative importance customers attach to certain criteria in their purchase decisions and to introduce new criteria. Influence over the criteria the customers use is the basis of enduring competitive advantage inside the customers' minds.

First to Market or First to Mind?

In a study of the innovation history of dozens of product categories over several decades, researchers asked the following question: do companies that are first to develop and bring a product to market have an enduring advantage in the product category they create? The study found that many pioneers fail. Companies that are first to market with a new product or technology do not have any significant advantage over followers in the marketplace. What's more, the current leaders in most markets are rarely the brands that pioneered the technology.[1] Instead, companies that were later entrants but that took the innovation to a mass market were much more likely to endure, with mass awareness and brands that became lasting market leaders. You probably don't use the Erwise web browser or the early search engines such as Excite or Galaxy, or the SixDegrees.com social network. And, very likely, you may have never heard of the MPMAN, the MP3 player from Saehan Information Systems of Korea. All of these products were on the market before the current market leaders, Google Chrome, Google Search, Facebook, and the iPod. Similarly, Pampers did not invent disposable diapers; nor was it the first on the market. The distinction for that technological leap belongs to Chux, a Johnson & Johnson brand. But Chux, like Erwise, Excite, SixDegrees.com, and the MPMAN, never made it to the mass market—it was a niche upmarket product in the 1960s when P&G developed and launched Pampers. Pampers built mass consumer awareness for the product and its brand, growing the diapers category from $10 million in 1966 to $370 million seven years later. And the P&G brand endures as the dominant player in the category that it has helped to grow to $30 billion annually, almost fifty years later.

In a choice between being first out of the lab or factory and being first to the customers' mind, the latter appears to be the strategy with the enduring advantage. Fast followers with a clear marketing strategy that builds a brand with strong associations to well-defined customer criteria of purchase tend to win over the long term. Products may be invented in the laboratory, but competitive advantage, it turns out, is seized in the marketplace. And a large part of the marketplace is the customers' minds.

Scoping Out the Playing Field

If you're the first brand in a product category to enter the customer's mind and you have your choice of a virgin field of criteria, where competitors have not yet arrived, which criteria should you pick to position your brand? Which will provide the most enduring advantage?

In any market, there are primary and secondary criteria. Primary criteria occupy the center of the playing field and usually relate to performance, power, efficacy, and speed—in functional categories, these criteria relate to the ability of the brand to get the job done. Secondary criteria include aesthetics (design, style), safety, and convenience. Of course, in aesthetic categories, such as jewelry or apparel, where form may supersede function, style and design may be the primary criteria, and performance (if it can even be defined independently of the primary criteria) becomes secondary. In yet other categories, such as child car seats, safety and convenience are primary criteria.

In any product category, customers find it easier to mentally associate each criterion with a single brand and to associate each brand generally with a single criterion. Customers cannot afford to clutter their mind space with multiple dominant brands for each criterion. Second and third brands in any product category must either play second fiddle or define their own criteria. The phenomenon is a simple result of people's memory limitations: you remember the name of the first person to cross the Atlantic on a solo flight, but do you remember the second? You remember the name of the fastest man on earth (the world record holder of the 100-meter sprint), but do you remember the name of the second-fastest?[2] Similarly, you remember that Volvo is associated with safety, but is there another automobile brand you associate with safety? Can you name a direct competitor brand to Jell-O? Finite cognitive capacity means that it is simply not efficient to have a second or third brand to occupy the same space. So being first to build the brand association to key criteria can in itself be a powerful and enduring advantage. Coca-Cola reentered China in 1979, just as economic reforms were taking place. Pepsi entered the market in 1981. Both cola companies gradually expanded coverage of the market, entering new provinces. Coca-Cola was first to enter some provinces, and Pepsi others. Decades later, the brand that had been first to the province was more likely to be the market leader in that province.

In the long term, however, there is more to building competitive advantage than being a squatter on preexisting criteria. Research on the formation of consumers' preference shows that brands that are first to establish strong associations in the customers' minds aren't merely associated with the primary dimensions; they actively define consumers' expectations and preferences on those dimensions. Such brands influence which criteria customers use, as well as the weight that customers give to those criteria in their decisions. Before Wrigley's came along, who knew how chewy chewing gum should be? Before Heinz, who knew how viscous ketchup should ideally be? Indeed, who cared that ketchup ought to be viscous? Before Google, who knew how relevant, meaningful, or fast search results should be? These dominant brands don't just position themselves on criteria. They define the criteria for the customer to use; they define what customers should be looking for, what people's expectations and the standard should be.

Later brands appearing on the market, regardless of their positioning, are compared with the first mover. Whether they like it or not, they are evaluated on the criteria defined by the dominant brand. And since the comparisons occur along dimensions that the dominant brand helped establish as criteria, keeping in mind its own superiority on those dimensions, later brands tend to come across as pale imitations or me-too players. They are harder to remember, and thus less likely to be considered, and then chosen.

In a set of pioneering academic studies conducted at Northwestern University's Kellogg School of Management, respondents were told of a new category of software that they were to evaluate.[3] Half the respondents were shown Brand A first, and the other half were shown Brand B first. Brand A was dominant on dimension X, while Brand B was dominant on dimension Y. The results showed that respondents who had seen Brand A first preferred it over Brand B, and vice versa. In other words, there was a pioneering advantage for the brand that was first to mind. But the really interesting results were that consumers' ideal points—what they considered their ideal combination of dimensions—shifted toward the brand they happened to have seen first, regardless of whether it was Brand A or Brand B. The dominant brand became the default for what a product in that space *ought to be*. Furthermore, the attributes or features associated with the brand respondents saw first became the more important criterion in their evaluation of brands they saw later. It is as though dominant brands acquire a gravitational field that pulls customer preferences toward the dominant brand. Later brands lack this gravitational pull. Such a mental attraction is the competitive advantage of brands that are first to define or capture criteria in the customer's mind.

In a study I recently conducted with my doctoral students, we examined what happens when a dominant brand in a product category introduces a radical new innovation. For example, what happens when Maytag or Whirlpool, considered the dominant brands in washing machines, introduces a waterless washing machine? When shown advertisements for these products, consumers came to see other competitor brands as less typical of the washing-machine category. The competitors were rated lower than they were before the innovation was introduced. Our results suggest that the dominant brand can shift consumer perceptions of the entire category by introducing a radical innovation. When a less dominant brand introduces the same innovation, there is no corresponding shift in the consumer evaluations of other brands. The dominant brand appears to be the only one with the power to shift the center of gravity of the category.

Dominance on a criterion also has significant advantages that play out over time. A dominant brand attracts new customers because it is at the center of its categories. In light of their results, Gregory Carpenter and Kent Nakamoto, the authors of the pioneering studies on the formation of consumer preference conclude that "the preference formation process produces a preference structure that makes the pioneer's market share invulnerable to competitors even if switching costs are minimal and brands can reposition."[4] In other words, brands that are the first to define customers' criteria for making a purchase in a category appear to have a license to draw the inside lines of the playing field on which they and other brands will compete. Our studies on the introduction of radical innovation suggest that players can redraw the lines even while the game is in progress.

In the baby diaper category, there is a significant amount of customer churn. Most new parents become customers for two to five years, depending on the number of children they have, and then exit the market, as a fresh set of new parents enters the market. Every year, the category loses at least 20 percent of its customers. At any given time, very few current customers have been in the market for more than five years. Despite this constant churn and intense competition, the brand market share of the market leader, Pampers, is relatively stable, at over 30 percent.

Pampers has high levels of awareness and visibility in the marketplace, so it tends to be the first in the consumers' mind. There, it helps define the criteria that matter to customers. Associating the brand with the primary functional criterion in the category, absorbency, builds an enduring competitive advantage. Competitors that claim similar performance on the same criterion tend to be seen as me-too imitations, lacking credibility or, at the very least, the ability to draw premium prices.

In sum, dominant brands are those that have established a strong association with a criterion of purchase. By convention and logic, early entrants tend to pick criteria that are primary in their product category. And even if an entrant chooses criteria that are not primary at the time, the criteria it chooses can become primary because the dominant brand picked them. A dominant brand has influence over the criteria that customers use and the weight they assign to those criteria, because it draws credibility from having been first to build the association and from considerable investments in advertising. These strengths underpin a lasting downstream competitive advantage. The lesson is, clearly, to build strong associations with a primary criterion of purchase and to do so early in the life cycle of a product category.

But not all players can be first. So what do you do if you are a later entrant into a category? If you find the primary criteria already occupied, what is your optimal strategy?

Challenging the Established Order

Unless a later entrant offers something extra, such as a powerful new feature or a lower price, the customer has little reason to switch from the incumbent brand to try an unfamiliar new one. The need to offer that something extra makes market entry costly for later entrants and may even deter some, further consolidating the competitive advantage of the dominant brand. But despite the risks of losing their distinctiveness and being overshadowed by the dominant brand, some later entrants nevertheless opt for a me-too strategy, positioning themselves as close substitutes, with little differentiation.

There are understandable, sometimes even optimal, reasons for this strategy. For example, the later entrant's market research suggests that this is where the center of gravity of customer preferences resides, so the latecomer finds it organizationally difficult or risky to do anything else. Another reason is that differentiation is technologically difficult, and imitation is an easier strategy. Or the latecomer's brand is a second fiddle anyway, and its economics are designed to generate a satisfactory margin playing in the shadow of the dominant player. The me-too brand recognizes that it may never get a large market share: its pricing, positioning, and quality will always be evaluated against the dominant brand. It will always be outspent by the dominant brand, and distributors, retailers, customers, and investors will always prefer the dominant brand. Despite these drawbacks, the market often needs a second player, even if just to avoid overreliance on a single supplier. What's more, the later entrant's lack of scale and its lower prices mean its margins are almost always lower than those of the leader. All of these outcomes are the result of a lack of influence over customers' criteria of purchase—me-too brands piggyback on the criteria created and dominated by the market leader. Despite this, some brands contentedly play in the me-too space and demonstrate that it is a viable space.

Still, a me-too position isn't the only opportunity open to later entrants. Second players willing to make investments in downstream advantage can attempt to define their own criteria of purchase. Secondary criteria are an obvious opportunity for differentiation. Second players often use safety, convenience, style, or design as criteria of purchase when the dominant brand has already occupied primary performance-related dimensions. Sometimes, by achieving parity on the primary criteria and emphasizing the importance of secondary criteria that favor the later entrant, an ambitious secondary player may even attempt to supplant the dominant player.

Consider the three players in the $5 billion erectile dysfunction drug market. Pfizer's Viagra, the first erectile dysfunction drug, took the market by storm when it was launched in April 1998, with a record six hundred thousand prescriptions filled that month alone. By the following month, surveys showed that 64 percent of adult Americans knew what Viagra was used for, a remarkable level of awareness for a newly introduced prescription pharmaceutical product.[5] After dispelling doubts about its safety (these doubts caused a sales dip early in the drug's life), the brand continued its stellar rise. The limited patent life of molecules and the potential entry of competitors spur pharmaceutical companies to maximize marketing and sales effort early in the life cycle of the product. At a price of $10 per dose and a gross margin of 90 percent, Viagra could afford to splurge on marketing and sales. Efforts included an annual advertising budget of up to $100 million, with patient-targeted television commercials in countries where the ads were allowed, and a sales push consisting of seven hundred thousand annual physician visits by Viagra salespeople.

By encouraging patients to discuss their symptoms with their physicians, the brand essentially built the market for erectile dysfunction where practically no market had existed before. Viagra became known as *the* solution for erectile dysfunction. The criterion of purchase it occupied was efficacy: it solved the problem; it got the job done. By 2001, Viagra's annual sales reached $1.5 billion, and there were still no competitors on the market, although it was clear that other pharmaceutical companies had taken note of the size, growth, and profitability of the market.[6]

In September 2003, Bayer, a German pharmaceutical company, launched the first competitor to Viagra, under the brand name Levitra. The Bayer product had a very similar profile to Viagra and was launched as a way of "enhancing the sexual experience." There were three strategic options open to Levitra. First, it could be positioned as superior to Viagra on the efficacy and performance dimensions. Second, it could be positioned as equally efficacious but with a better safety profile (although, of course, it would need credible and demonstrated claims to safety). Or third, it could be positioned as a me-too, offering a benefit similar to Viagra's, but at a slightly lower price. Nancy Bryan, a Bayer marketing executive, said that what patients wanted was "to improve the quality of their erections, to get one that's hard enough and lasts long enough for a satisfying sexual experience."[7] In other words, the dimension that Levitra hoped to occupy was the existing dimension of efficacy. Advertising expenditure for the brand stood in the $50 million to $75 million range, and the sales push was even greater than for Viagra. The product was priced slightly lower than Viagra.

In late 2003, Lilly Icos, a joint venture between pharmaceutical giant Eli Lilly and ICO, a biotech firm, brought the third brand, Cialis, to market. While the product formulation and efficacy of Cialis were similar to those of Viagra and Levitra, it was different in two ways. First, where the effects of Viagra and Levitra lasted four to five hours, Cialis offered a window of up to thirty-six hours to patients, which made it potentially much more convenient. Second, where some Viagra patients had complained of side effects of blue-tinted vision, Lilly Icos's product trials showed fewer sight-related side effects. Market research for Cialis showed that the key criteria for prescription among both urologists and primary care physicians were efficacy, followed by safety. These two criteria accounted for a relative importance of 70 percent. By comparison, duration had a relative importance of less than 10 percent.[8]

The strategic questions for Lilly Icos were whether these measures of relative importance were set in stone or whether physicians' criteria might be malleable. Would marketing the benefits of duration increase the criterion's importance in prescription and usage? Should Cialis be differentiated on its lack of side effects instead, given that safety was already one of the two most important criteria?

The positioning was hotly debated prior to launch. Eventually, the marketing campaign accompanying the launch of Cialis was designed to emphasize the benefits of duration. A dose was priced higher than a dose of Viagra—a move that further emphasized Cialis's superiority on the duration dimension, as well as underscoring the importance of the duration criterion itself. The higher price and the positioning meant that physicians and patients wanted to know what made Cialis "better" than Viagra. The answer was that duration provided many benefits, especially the ability to choose a time for intimacy in a thirty-six-hour window. Cialis marketing also distinguished the brand from Viagra with a softer positioning, emphasizing romance and intimacy rather than sex. Press reports described an early positioning study: "Viagra users who had been informed of the attributes of both drugs were given a stack of objects and asked to sort them into two groups, one for Viagra and the other for Cialis. Red lace teddies, stiletto-heeled shoes, and champagne glasses were assigned to Viagra, while fluffy bathrobes and down pillows belonged to Cialis."[9] Cialis was launched in late 2003, with an advertising budget that matched Pfizer's spending on Viagra.

The new criteria of purchase caught on gradually, through careful and painstaking physician and patient education and persistent marketing, but by 2012, Cialis passed Viagra's $1.9 billion in annual sales.[10] Through a decade-long marketing campaign, Cialis had succeeded in supplanting efficacy as the sole criterion of purchase in erectile dysfunction market by matching Viagra on that dimension and by making duration the criterion of choice for almost half the market.

The Brand Becomes the Criterion

Some companies aim even higher than associating their brand with the primary criterion of purchase or introducing new criteria of purchase and making them the dominant ones in their product category. They aim to make their brand the criterion of purchase.

Criteria are a useful organizing frame. By arranging available brands along one or two dimensions that matter to the customer, criteria help the customer simplify the complexity of the marketplace and the difficulty of choosing. There are hundreds of computer brands on the market, and each computer can be evaluated along hundreds of dimensions. Few buyers understand the technical specifications that make one computer better than another. But customers do know how to simplify the purchase of a complex machine. For a long time, one criterion, processor speed, stood above others in defining the personal-computer space. Expressed as a summary number initially in megahertz, then in gigahertz, it speaks to even technologically novice buyers about the relative quality of a computer. It is a simple, intuitive, and easy-to-use measure on which computers can be compared and ranked.

But there is a reason people use the processor speed of the chip, rather than other equally informative measures of performance or quality in evaluating computers. The reason lies in the history of the processor-chip industry and, in particular, with the marketing strategy of its leading firm, Intel. Thanks to Intel, chip speed became the measure that marks the progress of processor technology and is seen as the main indicator of the performance of a computer. You can hear the glee in Intel's statement when the company boasts, "Today many personal computer users can recite the specification and speed of the processor, just like car owners can tell you if they have a V4, V6 or V8 engine."[11]

This is not to say that speed is a perfect or complete measure of a computer's performance; far from it. Like any summary measure of a complex system, speed has its limitations: two computers with the same processor speed on their chips may perform very differently depending on the software loaded on the computer, the transfer speed of information to and from memory, its connectivity to the network, and many other variables. But most buyers of computers leave these intricacies to experts and rely instead on the simple summary measure of speed.

Upstream, Intel has pushed the development of faster chips since its founding in the late 1960s. Moore's Law, articulated in a 1965 paper by one of Intel's founders, Gordon Moore, noted that the number of components in integrated circuits had doubled every year since their invention in 1958 and would continue to double "for at least another ten years."[12] As it turns out, the doubling every twelve to eighteen months has continued for more than half a century, thanks in no small measure to Intel's R&D efforts.[13] Despite competitive challenges, Intel has maintained its speed lead over those decades.

Downstream, customers bought into speed as the defining measure of a computer's quality, and that development turned out to be very rewarding for Intel. It was as though the Toyota Prius had suddenly found that all car buyers around the world were now using environmental friendliness as their sole criterion of purchase. Intel's dominance on the speed dimension, combined with customers' preference for faster chips, has turned processor clock speed into a downstream competitive advantage, not just a technological feat or functional achievement that allows computer programs to run faster.

With its dominance on speed well established, both upstream and downstream, Intel attempted something even more audacious. Until the 1990s, customers who bought computers did not pay much attention to the chips that were inside, just as today's customers pay little attention to the brand of memory chips inside the computer or the processor chips inside their printers, phones, cars, game consoles, or washing machines. But the processor chip in the computer has become a critical criterion of choice thanks in large measure to the ubiquitous "Intel inside" marketing program, first launched in 1991.

The campaign was born after Dennis Carter, Intel's vice president for marketing, noticed that some retailers in Japan displayed computers with a handwritten "Intel in it" sign beside them. The processor chip is the brain of the computer. But it had generally remained anonymous and invisible to buyers of computers. Carter's team's marketing efforts had, until then, targeted the technical buyers of components at computer box makers such as IBM, HP, Dell, and the hundreds of smaller makers of PCs, rather than the end users of computers. Marketing to the end customer was seen as the job of these computer brands. But gradually, Carter and his team realized it made sense to target the end users because if Intel became a buying criterion, the box makers would be driven to use Intel chips and less likely to switch to rival chips. The idea of bringing the brand name of a chip that was buried deep inside the computer's guts to the outer layer and making it visible to the end customer in the prepurchase phase was the first step in turning the brand into a criterion of purchase.

The more customers recognized the chip's vital importance to the computer, the more they would use it as a criterion of purchase. Still, no hardware component manufacturer in the computer industry had ever attempted to brand its products for the end user. So Intel looked to other industries for successful examples. And it found several, including DuPont's Teflon in nonstick applications, Lycra in textiles, Gore-Tex for waterproof apparel, Shimano gears in bicycles, Dolby in audio systems, and NutraSweet artificial sweeteners in food and drinks. Each brand had shown that branding a component or an ingredient could turn the brand itself into a criterion of purchase. Each of these brands enjoyed a downstream competitive advantage that capitalized on its unique awareness among consumers.

Carter and his team devised the "Intel inside" campaign as a cooperative marketing program that initially gave computer assemblers and makers better advertising deals, provided the companies used the "Intel inside" logo on their print advertisements and on stickers affixed to their machines. An end-user marketing campaign, which in 1997 included a Super Bowl ad, was run to associate Intel with criteria such as leading technology, reliability, and safety and to make those criteria the important ones in customers' computer purchase decisions. These added reassurances were intended to turn the Intel brand, and its "Intel inside" logo, into a summary criterion encompassing the key dimensions of quality in a processing chip. If the Intel brand could come to stand for all of these dimensions, each dimension would not need to be individually occupied. Within six months of launch, three hundred PC makers had signed on to the "Intel inside" program, providing momentum to the brand building effort.

But not all computer makers were happy with the campaign. Some of Intel's largest customers, including IBM and Compaq, raised objections. Intel's campaign was leveling the playing field and diminishing the differentiation of their brands relative to no-name clone manufacturers. Customers were suddenly becoming more comfortable purchasing a machine from an unfamiliar computer box maker, provided it carried the "Intel inside" sticker. The Intel brand's tagline "the computer inside the computer" didn't sit well with IBM or Compaq, whose brand adorned the outside of the computer. Did customers really need two brands to provide them reassurance about the computer's quality? Some of the larger players could already see their market share fraying.

There were also detractors among observers both inside and outside the company.[14] "I think it's money down the drain," said Michael Murphy, editor of the California Technology Stock Newsletter.[15] Drew Peck of DLJ, a Wall Street investment bank, called it a "desperation move," and added that "chip companies were supposed to compete on technological excellence and not on advertising campaigns."[16] Despite customer and naysayer objections, Intel pressed on with the campaign.

In time, even the most reticent box makers overcame their objections to the "Intel inside" campaign. Those that recognized that their brand needed to add value over and above the brands of component suppliers such as Intel and Microsoft did better than those that failed to develop their own distinct and complementary value propositions.

Two very different but successful examples of differentiation are evident in the strategies of Apple and Dell. Apple's focus on design and the customer experience of the machine made the chip inside less important as a criterion of purchase—Apple customers buy their iMacs for the criteria that Apple has set out, including design and usability. The company did not even use Intel chips in its computers until 2006, and even after it switched to Intel chips, it never signed on to the "Intel inside" program. Dell chose a different path. It embraced the "Intel inside" campaign and chose to focus on the downstream criteria—on how the computer is purchased and delivered. Dell's position in the computer value chain is like that of a retailer selling branded goods: its sales process is designed to make buying a computer an easier and more customizable experience, and Intel's promise of a fast and reliable chip combines well with Dell's promise of an easy buy.

Intel's direct competitors, the other chip makers, also had to find their own responses to the success of the "Intel inside" campaign. Texas-based Cyrix essentially offered me-too chips at lower prices than Intel until it got bought out by National Semiconductor, which then repositioned the company's chip design efforts away from the PC space and avoided direct competition with Intel. Another competitor, AMD, was long viewed by computer manufacturers as a second source of supply for Intel-compatible processor chips because it used to make chips under license from Intel. Through the late 1990s, as the Intel brand became a criterion of purchase for end customers, AMD was squeezed. Volumes dropped as customers insisted that their computers carry an Intel chip. In response, in a long-shot bet, AMD attempted to leapfrog Intel on the speed dimension by developing the K-6, a chip that was faster than Intel's fastest Pentium chip on the market at that time. Perhaps AMD hoped to wrest control of the speed criterion from Intel, or perhaps its decision was merely technological chest thumping, which is more common than we think in the tech industry. But its victory was short-lived: within a few months of the launch of AMD's K-6, Intel launched the Pentium II and quickly reestablished speed supremacy. Customers continued to favor Intel, and AMD eventually positioned the K-6 as offering performance similar to Intel, at a cheaper price—a reversion to its classic me-too position.

At about the same time, another challenge was brewing for Intel. IBM, Motorola, and Apple combined forces to develop and launch the PowerPC chip, which was clocked at speeds faster than Intel's latest chips. At launch, the chip was met with initial enthusiasm by the engineering community. It looked like a serious contender. But end customers were unreceptive. They were insistent on "Intel inside," and when they did not find it on the PowerPC, they were uninterested. The PowerPC, unable to wrest control of the criteria of purchase from Intel, ended up leading a relatively anonymous existence inside Nintendo, PlayStation, and Xbox game systems. Despite their best technological efforts, none of the chip makers could break Intel's dominance of customers' criteria of purchase. None of the firms proved willing to make the investments in downstream brand building that would have been required to change the criteria away from speed to their own criterion of purchase. Intel held on to its dominance and to a gross margin that still hovers between 50 and 65 percent (compared with Apple's gross margin of just under 43 percent in early 2012).[17]

But what competitors could not accomplish, market evolution still might. In the late 2000s, as the PC gave way to tablets and phones as the principal browsing and communication devices, Intel's brand dominance began to be challenged. Smaller, nimbler manufacturers of chips had been searching for niche markets where they could compete without pitting themselves head-to-head against Intel. With the shift to mobile computing devices, the device makers' and end users' criteria of purchase changed from speed and reliability to mobility and low power consumption with high graphics capabilities—qualities that supported small but high-resolution screens. The smaller companies were quick to spot these opportunities. They developed chips with flexible processor configurations, so that only the parts of the chip that were being used were drawing power. Companies such as ARM in the United Kingdom, and NVIDIA in the United States have pushed the development of these new criteria and have benefited from the shift to mobile devices. But no chip maker has yet established the kind of dominance on criteria of purchase in the end-user market for mobile devices that Intel held for decades in the PC space. And Intel's full-force response to the rise of the mobile segment is yet to come. The game remains open, as no chip brand has, as yet, captured customers' criteria of purchase in mobile devices.

The Chicken or the Egg?

Looking at the "brandscapes" in many product categories, it is hard to say whether dominant brands are dominant because they fortuitously or strategically position themselves on a primary criterion, or whether the primary criteria become primary because the dominant brands make them so. The question in many a strategist's mind is as unresolved as the chicken-or-egg conundrum. Observation merely tells us that Tide is clean you can trust; that Intel, Google, and FedEx are dominant on processing speed in industries where speed matters; and that Samsonite is strong, lightweight, and durable in the luggage market, where strength, weight, and durability are essential. It does not answer the chicken-and-egg question of which comes first.

Can we envision a world where the primary criterion in the purchase of laundry detergent is not power or performance, but convenience and environmental friendliness? Or where computer chips, search engines, and courier services are evaluated not on speed but on convenience or service or low power consumption, or where luggage is evaluated on its maneuverability and color range? And if we could, would it be a world populated by the same or a different set of brands? In other words, do brands make criteria salient for consumers, or do brands merely position themselves on salient criteria? This question is not merely academic; it is strategically important. Managers want to know whether it is criterion *selection* (choosing the right criterion) that will win them competitive advantage or whether it is criterion *investments,* where regardless of the choice of criteria, their marketing skill can make any criterion important. The question is also interesting beyond strategy. It gets to the heart of an age-old marketing question: does marketing serve preexisting customer needs, or does it help create them?

A clue comes from some firms' ability to create criteria that are otherwise trivial, irrelevant, or meaningless and turn them into decisive criteria for customers, as well as from research that shows that these criteria can be important in differentiation, consumer evaluations, and choice. Take, for example, shampoo that contains vitamins or even silk, or beer that is advertised as "beechwood aged," or coffee that is differentiated by its "flaked crystals."[18] In each instance, a criterion that is objectively irrelevant or meaningless for the quality of the product is promoted by the seller, and adopted by the buyer, as meaningfully differentiating a brand from its competitors. The irrelevant criterion makes the brand unique and gives it advantage. To the extent that customers use such criteria in their decisions, the practice demonstrates that marketers have the ability to create criteria out of thin air—to create needs or, at least, preferences.

In some categories, all brands share the irrelevant criterion, which consumers use to determine the relative value of offerings within the category. For example, consumers evaluate digital cameras using the simple summary measure of megapixels, when in fact the megapixel measure has little to do with the quality of pictures taken by the camera. It is the size of the light sensor rather than the megapixel count that determines picture quality.[19] Similarly, automobile buyers often rely on horsepower as a measure of the muscle of a car, when it is actually torque they are looking for, as torque determines acceleration, which is the sensation drivers seek. Customers rely on thread count when buying synthetic bed sheets, but thread count is irrelevant in synthetic fabrics—it only provides a measure of quality for natural fibers such as cotton. These irrelevant criteria become meaningful in part because they are advertised. "They wouldn't be advertising it if it weren't a selling point," the consumer reasons. There must be a reason yogurt is advertised as containing ten billion bacteria: ten billion must be better than five billion; otherwise, they wouldn't be proclaiming it on the tub. Irrelevant attributes may even become defining criteria for the entire industry. They define the playing field on which a meaningless and futile arms race takes place. Except that it is no longer meaningless and futile if customer behavior depends on it and if customers are willing to pay more for a product with more of the irrelevant attribute.

The widespread use of trivial or irrelevant criteria can become frustrating for some brand owners. For example, how do you build and sell a better-quality camera with a bigger light sensor, or any other attractive features, when all consumers care about is the megapixel count? Because other criteria matter less, consumers aren't as willing to pay for them. Once a criterion such as megapixels becomes entrenched, brands have little choice but to match competitors on the pixel count while trying to appeal to the more savvy customers (e.g., professional photographers) or niche customers (e.g., sports photographers) with more relevant criteria and a more nuanced message about picture quality.

Ultimately, however, the strategic question boils down to this: are you a criterion maker or a criterion taker? Can you increase the importance that customers attach to criteria that favor your brand over those of competitors? Can you introduce new criteria into the lexicon and the purchase routines of customers? Or do you position yourself along criteria that competitors and customers already use? Clearly, there are strategic benefits to creating your own criteria and increasing the importance of criteria that naturally favor you. You are seen as unique, you have fewer competitors, and you have a long-term association with those criteria. But keep a look out for a whole different type of criterion that can upend the game in your product category. Every once in a while, society-wide criteria emerge and wash over multiple product categories. These can be opportunities to drive business growth and build new brands. We'll call these *meta-criteria*.

Meta-Criteria

We've seen some criteria of purchase that are associated with brands and other criteria that define product categories. Some criteria of purchase are even larger than product categories. They are part of the zeitgeist. They affect consumer behavior across many product categories. Examples include environmental friendliness, fair trade, health and wellness, and local production. While the introduction or importance of these criteria cannot be controlled by any single brand, all brands are subject to their influence. Whether you like it or not, your brand will be evaluated on these criteria by certain segments of the market. And depending on both the importance attached to the criteria and the size of the segment, these meta-criteria will influence your market positioning and your market share.

Toyota's 1997 (Japanese) launch of the Prius, a hybrid electric vehicle that is rated one of the cleanest cars in terms of its emissions, was intended to benefit from the emerging consumer criterion of environmental friendliness. The car was rolled out to global markets in 2000 and has since sold almost three million vehicles. Even as other car manufacturers have launched hybrid cars, pushing the clean-burning vehicle segment to sales of about half a million vehicles a year in the United States in 2012, the Prius remains the dominant player. In fact, as more consumers switch to green criteria, the first brand of vehicle they consider is the Prius. This is not to say that Toyota has forgone production or sales of its gas-guzzling Land Cruisers. But its Prius brand has built a formidable competitive advantage on an emerging criterion of purchase. The brand benefits from a rising tide of consumer environmental consciousness, which means that associating the Prius brand with environmentally clean vehicles makes its marketing efforts more efficient. The green market still represents a small share of the overall car market. But as it grows, the Prius is well placed to be to that market what Heinz is to ketchup and what Coca-Cola is to the cola category.

For similar reasons, sellers in many other product categories keep an eye on emerging and niche criteria and adapt their offerings to capture opportunities along these criteria or to stave off competitors that may use the new criteria as entry points. Many coffee retailers, including Starbucks and Costa Coffee, carry a fair-trade option to cater to customers who prefer their cappuccino guilt-free. In the food industry, meta-criteria of purchase noticeably shifted from primarily taste to "better for you" and are now moving toward functional therapeutic claims. In response, many grocery retailers and food manufacturers first developed organic, low-sugar, low-fat, and low-salt options to serve customers using the better-for-you criterion and are now highlighting added vitamins, calcium, omega-3 fatty acids, and antioxidants as key dimensions of their products.

It pays to monitor macrotrends because an emerging meta-criterion can be an opportunity to position your brand to capitalize on it, as Toyota did with the Prius, but it can also be a potential threat, depending on your existing brands' positions. An issue that goes viral over the Internet can rapidly become a criterion of purchase. In late 2003, Kraft Foods was taken aback when the trans-fat content of food products suddenly emerged as a negative criterion of purchase (consumers were turning away from foods that contained trans fat) and when its Oreo cookie brand consequently became the lightning rod for disgruntled consumers. A lawsuit filed by a consumer group in California sought to compel Kraft to stop selling Oreo cookies to children until Kraft could ensure that Oreos contained no trans fats. Responding to the new criteria of purchase, by early 2005 the company reformulated 650 food products in its line to eliminate or reduce trans fats.[20]

Is a Criterion Advantage Sustainable?

Once your brand establishes an association with a criterion of purchase, is the advantage durable? Kodak built mass awareness for photography and photographic film and dominated the market for much of the twentieth century. Its downstream competitive advantage resided in its near synonymy with photography, in its ubiquitous distribution presence, and in its retail relationships. Memories became Kodak moments.

Consequently, the company was well placed to make the transition to digital photography, as customers would have followed Kodak. And as we have seen, the company's R&D labs were home to landmark technological developments in digital photography, including the first ever charge-coupled device in 1975 and the first camera-size megapixel sensor in 1986.[21] But the company failed to tilt.

Digital photography was seen as a threat to the company. Too rapid a transition to the new technology would put at risk the investments, revenues, margins, retailer relationships, and business model the company had so successfully built in film. Risk aversion and unwillingness to kill its old business contributed to the company's protectiveness of its film business as the world went digital without Kodak. Eventually, Kodak lost its downstream advantage, trying to cling to its shrinking upstream advantage. Its brand remained indelibly associated with film as other brands such as Lexar, Sony, Canon, Nikon, and SanDisk came to claim associations with digital photography and rapidly developed their own criteria of purchase in the digital space.

One consequence of the strong association of a brand with a criterion of purchase is that even when the brand falls behind technologically or fails to deliver on the product, it continues to benefit from customers' default assumptions for a long while. Its downstream advantage carries it even when the upstream lags. Customer associations provide the brand with a buffer that shields it from crises and quality issues. Customers are slow to switch, so that even if decline sets in, it is gradual, allowing the company time to fix the problem and respond to challenges.

Brands die hard. Microsoft was able to retain most of its customers even through the life of the ill-conceived Windows Vista operating system, a disastrous product that would have been the death knell for a start-up brand. Apple's reputation was barely dented despite the antenna problems of the iPhone 4, AT&T's spotty coverage, and the embarrassment of prematurely launching Siri, an artificial intelligence bot that was not quite ready for prime time, and faulty Apple Maps. The brand easily weathered these slipups. Sometimes, the downstream advantage provides so much of a buffer against competition, that it can lead the company to complacency: it allows managers the room they need to remain in denial about challengers and challenges. When BlackBerry sales continued to rise, even into 2012 in some parts of the world, its newly appointed CEO felt free to declare early that year, "We have fantastic devices in a fantastic ecosystem. I don't think there is some drastic change needed."[22]

One means by which dominant firms maintain their downstream advantage is by viewing their innovation efforts through the lens of criteria of purchase. Rather than develop products and incorporate new features into their products because the companies have the technology, they develop products and features that strengthen their association with the criteria of choice. New products and features help to evolve the meaning of the criteria in the customers' minds. Take Volvo's long-standing association with safety. It is no accident that Volvo was the first brand to introduce laminated glass windshields (1944), three-point seat belts (1959), antilock brakes (1984), side-impact protection systems (1995), and pedestrian detection with autobrake (2010) as standard equipment on its cars, along with many other safety innovations. Each introduction is accompanied by a marketing campaign that reminds customers of Volvo's safety credentials. The innovations and the campaigns reinforce the association of the brand with safety in the customers' minds and strengthen the importance of safety in their purchase decisions. Years later, Volvo's innovations often become standard equipment mandated by law. Yes, this equalizes the product playing field, but by then, Volvo has reinforced its safety credentials in customers' minds and is busy redefining customer's expectations of safety with some new feature that other cars will in time emulate. Kodak could have learned from Volvo's tactics.

A second way in which dominant firms maintain their competitive advantage in the marketplace is by fragmenting the market according to criteria of purchase they help define. Take Nike's dominance of the athletic-shoe market. Whether the criterion is the distinction between court shoes and off-court shoes, the distinction between trail shoes and track shoes, shoes directed at specific sports such as kayaking, or shoes for runners who prefer to run shoeless, the brand has been at the forefront of defining why consumers buy athletic shoes. Performance remains the overarching and unifying theme for the brand, but within each sport, Nike defines the criteria of purchase through specific design features in its shoes. It fragments the market because different customers buy for different reasons. And in fragmenting the market, Nike contains competitors to small niches, preventing the firms from threatening the whole brand. It would be hard for an upstart to offer the entire range of shoes that Nike sells. Fragmentation also raises the barriers for other, large competitors, such as Adidas: retailers and consumers demand a product range similar to Nike's. Nike's constant definition of new criteria forces competitors to play catch-up, turning them into me-too players. This makes it less likely that a competitor will emerge to challenge Nike in the way that Cialis challenged Viagra. And if one does, Nike will be quick to thwart it, either by offering a direct competitor product or by buying the rival, as it did with the soccer-specific Umbro brand.

The Criteria of Purchase Checklist

- ✓ Which criteria does your brand occupy in the customers' minds?
- ✓ How strongly is your brand associated with the criteria of purchase?
- ✓ How important are these criteria in the marketplace? Does a large proportion of customers use the criteria?
- ✓ How much weight do your criteria carry in customers' decisions?
- ✓ Are you a first mover on the criteria you occupy, or a follower or me-too company?
- ✓ Are there criteria that remain open in your product category? Are there criteria that customers do not yet use but that could be important in their decision making?

- ✓ Are you defensively preempting the coverage of criteria by launching line or product extensions?
- ✓ If you are a later entrant, are you consciously choosing between a differentiated and a me-too strategy?
- ✓ In pursuing a differentiated strategy, are you matching the dominant brand on its criterion before differentiating on yours?
- ✓ Is your brand a criterion of purchase in the category? Could it be?
- ✓ What are you doing to maintain your downstream competitive advantage of brand associations with criteria of purchase?
- ✓ What are the emerging criteria of purchase in your category? Do you have a strategy for covering those criteria through line or brand extensions, or new brands?
- ✓ Which emerging meta-criteria could affect your category? Are these threats or opportunities?
- ✓ How do your upstream activities contribute to reinforcing your downstream advantage on criteria of purchase?
- ✓ How do you use feature and product innovation to reinforce and sustain your position on key criteria of purchase?

8. Knowing Who Your Competitors Are

The deep dive into the customer's mind in chapter 6 laid out the outside boundary (cognitive economy), and chapter 7 examined the inside lines (criteria of purchase) on the playing field in the customers' mind. Building on the metaphor, we will now examine the rules of the game.

Without competitors, there would be no game. You and your competitors are vying for ideal locations in customers' minds, customers' attention, and, ultimately, customers' consideration and choice. The competition for real-world resources (whether it is media, shelf space, raw materials, or talent) is a mere proxy for the real battle for the customers' cognitive resources. To win the battle for a piece of the customer's mind, you must understand the rules by which the mind stores and processes information about you and your competitors.

Let's begin with a question: who are your competitors? Take a minute to list them. Once you have a list of two, three, or four competitors you consider your closest rivals, ask yourself how you know. How do you know these are your competitors? Are they the companies that most often pitch for business alongside yours? Are they the brands that sit beside yours on the shelf? Are they the offerings that appear near your brand on search-page rank? Are they the firms that compete with you for resources and employees? Are they the firms that compete with you for the consumer's dollar? If the company or brand is your competitor, then the answer is yes for at least some of these questions. But ultimately, only one condition determines whether your competitor belongs on the list: whether your target customers include the competitor among the brands they choose or at least consider. Consideration and choice occur in the customer's mind.

So let's ask this question with a downstream tilt. Instead of asking which brands you consider your competitors, ask which brands the customer considers before making a choice. Now instead of mentally scrambling to come up with a list, you have to find a way to get into the customers' mind. This is not easy, but is worth doing, because your list and the customers' may not be the same. Invariably, the list inside the customer's mind is more relevant and indicative of your true competition than the one you prepare in the comfort of your office. A customers' list may contain surprises. Is it possible, for example, that a significant competitor for Omega's $3,000 Swiss watches is a Nikon camera? Would managers at either Omega or Nikon have considered the other brand a significant competitor? Are their competitive strategies explicitly designed to take into account competitors in a different product category? They should be, because it appears that these brands do compete closely. Many online retailers now provide the shopper with a list of products that other customers purchased or viewed after the shopper viewed the original item. According to Amazon.com, customers who bought an Omega Seamaster watch were indeed also likely to spend time viewing a Nikon D800 single-lens reflex camera (also priced at about $3,000).

Playing in the Consideration Set

The products and brands the customer considers before purchasing yours are your competitors. The products and brands the customer purchases after considering yours are also your competitors. Both sets of products and brands are critically important. Of all the products and brands available to fulfill a given need, the customer will generally consider fewer than a handful before choosing one to buy, even in the most elaborate of purchasing scenarios. This handful of brands is the consideration set—your closest competitors. Brands in the consideration set are evaluated on fewer than a handful of criteria before one is ultimately chosen for purchase. Before we get into a more detailed understanding of the purchase process, consider three critical questions about competitive strategy from the marketer's perspective:

1. How do you make sure your brand is among the set of brands considered for purchase by the customer?
2. How do you ensure that there are as few brands as possible in the consideration set, for as many people as possible? How do you make sure your brand is one of those?
3. Finally, which other brands are in the consideration set, and how do you make sure your brand is the one chosen for purchase from among those?

Now let's delve a little deeper into the consumers' mental process to understand how you can systematically increase your chances on each of the three strategic questions.

Gaining Entry into the Consideration Set

To address the questions, let's return to the central idea of criteria of purchase. Associating your brand with criteria of purchase is only the first step in influencing customer behavior. An important next step is to understand and influence how customers use these criteria of purchase. According to marketing researchers' account of buyer behavior, customers simplify the large set of available alternatives to the much-smaller consideration set by applying rules of thumb that use certain criteria as cutoffs or must-haves.[1] Any of the following, for example, could be a cutoff criterion for consumers forming consideration sets before choosing an automobile: must have six seats and room for the dog, must be a hybrid, must be priced below $25,000, must be made domestically, must be German, must get at least thirty highway miles per gallon, and must be easy to parallel park. These cutoff criteria are so pervasive that car companies often define the target segments by customers' cutoff criteria: the large-vehicle segment, the environmentally friendly segment, the price-conscious segment, the domestic segment, the German-car-enthusiast segment, the fuel-efficient segment, and the urban-car segment. Under this definition, a segment is a set of consumers who are sufficiently convinced by a given criterion to use it as a cutoff in forming their consideration set.

Your first strategic goal, then, is to convince as large a segment of the market as possible to use cutoff criteria that favor your brand. Sure, German car brands compete with each other, but they also have a collective interest in ensuring that a significantly large segment of consumers continues to be sufficiently fascinated by the mythology of German engineering to use that as a cutoff criterion in forming their consideration set. A look at the chat boards of German-car enthusiasts shows that to this customer segment, a Lexus, an Infiniti, an Acura, and all luxury Japanese car brands simply do not compare with the solidity and drivability of a German-made Mercedes, BMW, Porsche, or Audi. The simplifying heuristic of "German" makes the consumer's decision much easier because it eliminates a large swath of available brands that are irrelevant to this segment's choice. So convinced is this segment of the superiority of German engineering that year after year, the group willingly ignores the *Consumer Reports* testing results that place Japanese brands such as Honda, Infiniti, and Subaru higher on both drivability and reliability. Members of this segment also dismiss the annual customer satisfaction and reliability ratings, reported by J.D. Power and Associates, that show German brands lagging, and they accept the higher annual cost of owning a German vehicle. The marketer of German brands could not hope for a better cutoff criterion or a more convinced set of customers. After all, BMW's marketing managers would much rather limit their competitive set to Mercedes, Audi, and Porsche than compete with a much larger set of brands. One benefit of comparisons with these brands is that it improves BMW's relative value per dollar than would a comparison with a broader set of less expensive brands.

The Volkswagen brand, positioned by marketers and long seen by customers as an economy brand in the United States, has at times attempted to benefit from the German-only segment's awe of German engineering by emphasizing its German roots. The "German" association is Volkswagen's entry ticket into the consideration set—after all, Volkswagen is the largest German car manufacturer, outproducing all the other brands combined. But membership in the consideration set is not the same as production numbers. The brand would benefit if consumers included Volkswagen in their list of German cars, as many of the associations of solidity and drivability from that category would rub off on the brand, overcoming earlier associations that tended toward economy.

Close the Door Behind You

As a member of a consideration set, you have a second strategic imperative: to ensure that membership of the set remains as exclusive as possible. A smaller consideration set means fewer competitors and, hopefully, less intense competition. In a study of computer purchasers, I found that consumers who bought an iMac considered 2.11 brands, while consumers who bought a Windows-based PC considered 3.35 brands prior to purchasing the one they bought. The cutoff criteria that led consumers to consider an iMac were based on its differentiated positioning (its use of a different operating system, its emphasis on design and usability, and its higher price). Using these as cutoff criteria automatically eliminates numerous competitors and leaves the iMac playing in a much smaller consideration set than Windows-based PCs. Similarly, buyers of the Mini have a much smaller consideration set than do buyers of a Honda Civic, because Civic buyers also consider the Toyota Corolla, the Ford Focus, the Chevrolet Cruze, the Hyundai Elantra, the Mazda 3, the Nissan Sentra, the Volkswagen Golf, and others. Buyers of the Mini, in contrast, have often already convinced themselves that it's the car they want before they begin their car research.

One way to make the cutoff more exclusive is to convince consumers to raise the bar on the cutoff criteria they use, leaving competitors that do not or cannot match the new standard stranded outside the consideration set. Consider the arms race on the cutoff criteria of which generation a smartphone belongs to. Consumers are aware of a correlation between the generation of the network (the G) and network data transfer speeds, but the real meaning of the Gs plays out in the competitive battle. Smartphone manufacturers must match the latest cutoff criteria or risk being left out of the game. Few consumers today would consider buying a 2G or even a 3G, which was the standard a couple of years ago. And given the pace of development in network technology, the cutoff continues to rise, with criteria such as LTE (long-term evolution, a network technology that speeds up data transfers) setting new standards. The arms race along these customer criteria accounts for the R&D investments that companies make and the constant product-development treadmill on which they find themselves.

But a technological lead becomes a downstream competitive advantage only if customers use the distinctive technological feature as a criterion of purchase. Otherwise, it is just an interesting technological quirk, and your investments in its development are either merely a means of staying in the game or unlikely to have the returns you expected. For companies that tilt, the goal is to develop technological features that competitors cannot easily replicate and that customers will use as criteria to eliminate numerous alternatives from their consideration set.

Now, if you've gotten this far, you've probably been paying attention, so you might have noticed that the two strategic imperatives discussed so far are likely to be at odds with each other. On the one hand, you want to convince the largest possible segment of consumers to use your cutoff criteria. On the other hand, you want to limit the number of brands entering the consideration set. The more "exclusive" a cutoff you use, the fewer the people who are likely to use it. Thanks to this trade-off, the marketer's strategic options are often framed as a choice between a niche-player approach (e.g., an iMac and a Mini), so that you contend with fewer competitors inside the consideration set, and a wider-market approach (e.g., a Dell computer and a Honda Civic) but with the concomitant burden of more competitors. The choice is worth heeding because most brands are successful by choosing one or the other approach in that trade-off.

But many breakthrough products and brands share a common characteristic: they shred the trade-off. They convince large numbers of customers that their brand or product is so differentiated that no other brands can be considered in the same set. Brands such as the Walkman, the iPod, the iPhone, Red Bull, Swatch, Beanie Babies, Häagen Dazs, the Wii, Gillette blades, and Walmart have their cake and eat it too: they appeal to a large market and simultaneously ensure a small consideration set. Intel, as we saw in the previous chapter, ensured that the brand itself became the cutoff criterion for PC chips through its "Intel inside" campaign, with the result that it very often played in a consideration set of one, while appealing to a mass market.

Who Else Is in the Consideration Set?

The third strategic move for marketers is to influence not just the size of the consideration set, but also its composition. In other words, you get to influence who else gets into the consideration set with you. Yes, you have a say in who you compete with. The Honda automobile website, like those of many manufacturers, helpfully provides visitors with a comparison tool that allows them to benchmark the Civic with competitor brands such as the Toyota Corolla, the Chevrolet Cruze, and the Ford Focus, but, crucially, not the Hyundai Elantra, the Nissan Sentra or Versa, or the Mazda 3. The absence of the Nissan and Mazda brands may be attributed to their small market shares, but the Elantra's absence is conspicuous because it is the most serious challenger to the Civic's market-leading position. Honda does not include the Elantra in its suggested comparison set, presumably to reduce the likelihood of the competitor car's inclusion in consumers' consideration sets. Of course, consumers today can find comparisons of any combination of products on websites if they make the effort. But by presenting their product judiciously, sellers can influence which products are actually compared—which products consumers will make the effort to compare.

The second, third, or fourth players in a market sometimes use comparative advertising that pits them in a contest against the leading brand and from which they emerge the victor. This type of comparative advertising serves three purposes. First, it attempts to limit the consideration set to the two brands compared. Second, it raises consumer awareness (and use) of the criterion on which the comparison takes place (which presumably favors the challenger). Finally, it allows the challenger to piggyback on the awareness of the leading brand to introduce a lesser-known brand into the consideration set of consumers who might not otherwise be aware of the brand or would not have considered it. The market leader rarely engages in comparative advertising. Because its brand is already well known and belongs in the consideration set, its focus is on reinforcing the criteria that customers are already using. Comparative advertising is a tool favored by challenger brands that use it to enter the consideration set and to close the door behind them so that other brands do not enter.

Efforts to influence the composition of the consideration set are not limited to communication tools. Automobile manufacturers and dealers have made significant efforts to maintain a brand-based dealership structure, in which dealers sell only noncompeting brands, and have resisted moves toward independent car superstores that carry multiple competing brands of cars. As a result, the car buyer rarely gets to do a side-by-side comparison of the cars. He or she may also be deterred from comparing too many cars, because of the time and cost involved in visiting multiple dealerships. The same logic is evident in many other industries. Take Häagen Dazs, the super-premium ice cream brand. The brand offers retailers dedicated Häagen Dazs–branded display freezers in which, by agreement, only Häagen Dazs ice cream is displayed. These freezers limit comparison with other brands: once the consumer has opened the freezer door, he or she decides between the banana split, vanilla bean espresso, and dulce de leche flavors of the Häagen Dazs brand and is much less likely to consider other brands.

Trade-Offs and Exchange Rates

Once your brand is inside the consideration set, the competitive game changes. Customers use their criteria not as hard cutoffs, but to make trade-offs. Their information-processing goal is no longer to eliminate brands that do not fit their needs, but to pick the one that fits best. Inside the consideration set, with just a few brands to consider, customers engage in the more complex task of evaluating multiple criteria simultaneously, trading off price for reliability, roominess for style, sportiness for comfort, and so on. The use of trade-offs means that the brand the customer eventually chooses is not necessarily one that dominates on all criteria (there are very few brands or products that do), but rather one that offers the best compromise across the criteria used inside the consideration set.

Your first goal as a marketer is to ensure that once inside the consideration set, you *understand* which criteria are important to customers and the exchange rate the customers use in their trade-offs. How much fuel efficiency will customers trade off for greater roominess in a vehicle? Understanding customers' trade-offs allows you to tailor your products and messages to those trade-offs. Knowing that roominess is more important than fuel efficiency to the family segment allows you to emphasize roominess in product design, in brochures, and in sales pitches. But as discussed in the previous chapter, understanding and reacting to the consumer's trade-offs is helpful, but you need more than this passive approach.

So the second goal of marketing inside the consideration set is to influence the trade-offs that consumers make. The competitive task here is essentially to increase the *relative* importance of attributes associated with your brand as well as the perceived value of your brand on these attributes. As we have seen, brand managers for Cialis challenged Viagra for market leadership by changing the relative importance of duration as a criterion of purchase for patients and physicians and then by demonstrating their brand's unequivocal superiority on this dimension.

Let's consider an example. If you're Volvo, you may have convinced a segment of consumers to use a very high safety standard as a cutoff criterion—a standard that leaves only Volvo in the consideration set. This is Volvo's core segment of consumers. But for many other consumers, the cutoff criterion for safety is lower and is thus met by several brands, all of which enter the consideration set. Inside this set, other criteria come into play. Volvo brand managers would like to ensure that these consumers use a very high exchange rate for the safety dimension when considering the other criteria. The managers want consumers to be reluctant to trade safety for any other criteria, so that the buyers are even willing to accept less-than-optimal styling or fuel efficiency in exchange for an enhanced feeling of safety.

If you're BMW, on the other hand, you want to turn safety into a basic cutoff criterion in the consideration set. Brand managers would aim to make safety no longer relevant in the consideration set, because all cars inside this set meet the requisite safety norms. BMW would prefer that inside the consideration set, consumers evaluate cars on criteria such as driving dynamics, styling, and pleasure. At BMW's very successful day-long driver training courses, where customers (and soon-to-be customers) learn about driving from professional race car and rally drivers, for example, the trainers begin by underscoring both safety principles and the safety of the BMW vehicle. They then spend much of the rest of the day in hands-on demonstrations of the handling prowess and driving dynamics of BMW vehicles. The higher the value that consumers attach to these latter criteria, the less willing they will be to trade them off against other criteria and the more likely they will choose the BMW brand from among the brands in the consideration set.

Customer Involvement

This account of the customer buying process so far describes how the customer funnels the available brands through criteria to arrive at a consideration set and, from there, uses trade-offs on multiple criteria to make a choice. I've emphasized the strategic importance of associating your brand with a criterion of purchase and increasing the importance of those criteria in the customers' decision making. This sound reasoning works well for high-involvement product categories in which the customer makes the effort to elaborately process marketplace information about brands and criteria. But for the billions of low-involvement purchase decisions that consumers make every day, more basic processes such as the customer's ability to remember brand-related information may matter just as much to determining whether a brand is considered and chosen. In these product categories, not all brands available on the market are even in the running to make it into the consideration set—some may not even be remembered. If a brand is never recalled, none of its painstakingly constructed associations with purchase criteria will be evoked. It simply won't matter. Memory processes matter because many purchase decisions are made in the absence of a complete list of available brands. Memory is often about context. As are many downstream activities.

Because the customers' consideration of a brand is subject to the whims of their memory, the consideration set is also fluid. The brands that customers remember will depend on the situation (you can remember some things in context, but not out of context), so the consideration set is not stable—it can consist of a different set of brands on different occasions. The brands of ice cream the consumer considers purchasing when making his or her shopping list may be different from the brands the same person considers when in front of the ice cream freezer. For these low-involvement purchases, contextual cues such as location-based mobile advertising, point-of-sale promotion, and distinctive packaging can dramatically alter the likelihood of your brand's entering the consideration set at the right time.

Contextual cues can insert a brand into a consideration set when it otherwise might not have been remembered. They can also exclude competitor brands from consideration when the competitors might otherwise have been included. Research shows, for example, that recall of certain brands may be inhibited when other brands are presented as cues. In psychological studies, subjects recall a smaller proportion of the forty-two or forty-four remaining states, if given a subset (say, six or eight) of the fifty as cues, than the proportion of the fifty they can recall if they're not given any as cues to get them started. A similar effect occurs when a subset of brands in a category is presented and the respondents are asked to list the remaining brands in the category.[2]

The marketing implication of saturation-level point-of-sale advertising is adopted by many low-involvement brands. Procter & Gamble, for example, spends about half of its $10 billion US advertising budget in-store rather than on media. It is no surprise that low-involvement products are among the most heavily advertised products. These include companies that sell products such as soap, drinks, shampoo, regularly consumed food items, and telecom services. The products in these industries themselves may be inherently indistinguishable from those of their competitors, so the competitive game is about saturation and repetitive advertising. In and of itself, this saturation advertising may appear to be giving the brand merely a tactical advantage: it sways a percentage of sales toward Coca-Cola just as the customer is making a decision. Perhaps the advantage would even disappear if the point-of-sale advertising were removed, offering no lasting advantage. But meta-analysis of research on mere exposure shows that even when consumers are unaware of having seen ads for a brand, they like brands they've been exposed to.[3] When aggregated across millions of points of sale, saturation advertising also acts as a significant barrier to entry for competitors. And holding on to critical advertising locations (whether real or virtual) where consideration sets are formed or choices are made prevents competitors from capturing those locations.

The need to provide contextual cues doesn't just influence marketer's decisions about where to advertise; it should also influence what is communicated in the advertisements. Whether it is a beer brand building associations with beaches, bikinis, and bacchanalia, or a toothpaste brand associating itself with a celebrity, when marketers think of building brand associations, their focus is to get consumers to think of its benefits or to simply create a positive feeling. Marketers hope that when the consumer thinks of the brand, those benefits or positive associations will automatically come to mind, increasing the likelihood of the brand's being chosen. In other words, a marketer spends a considerable amount of time creating the associations that come to the consumers' mind when they think of the brand. But research suggests that an equally important goal for the marketer should be to flip the question around and ask, what associations evoke the brand? Flipping the question means that the marketer can increase the likelihood that every time the consumer thinks of diet, grocery shopping, or afternoon thirst, Diet Pepsi pops into mind, turning these contextual cues into memory jogs for the brand. Development of those associations with Diet Pepsi requires repeated activation and rehearsal. Repeat and reminder advertising is common in low-involvement product categories, but it traditionally has been intended to build associations evoked by the brand rather than associations that evoke the brand. An ingenious exception is Wrigley's recent advertising campaign that asks, "What you gonna chew when they come for you?"

The rules of the competitive playing field spell out how brands compete for the consumers' consideration, choice, and loyalty. To break into the consideration set, your brand must meet the cutoff on the key criteria that customers use. If the criteria are unique to your brand or the cutoff is so high that only your brand makes it into the consideration set, you minimize competition by limiting the brands that enter the set. If you can persuade large numbers of customers to use the unique or high bar, you have a winning combination of a large segment and few competitors. If you enter the consideration set along with other brands, your competitive objective is to maximize your chances of being selected for purchase from within the set. You do this by maximizing the relative exchange rate between your brand's key positioning criteria and those of your competitors—by increasing the importance of your criteria relative to the competitors' criteria for as many customers as possible.

Once your brand is chosen, your focus shifts to building customer loyalty. Traditional marketing prescriptions for building loyalty include investments in customer satisfaction and higher levels of service. The prescriptions presented here are different. The recommendations include building a sustainable business by understanding the cognitive processes that lead to loyalty: brand momentum, customers' tendency to seek information that confirms rather than disconfirms their beliefs and their behavior, a bias toward the status quo rooted in loss aversion, and habit. Each of these has a powerful influence on repurchase behavior, which explains why downstream competitive advantage, once established, tends to be enduring. Chapter 10 discusses in detail why downstream competitive advantage is sustainable for businesses that tilt.

The Customer Mental Processing Checklist

- ✓ Which cutoff criteria do customers use to consider purchases in your product category?
- ✓ What are the cutoff criteria you would like your customers to use?
- ✓ Which companies or brands are your principal competitors inside your consumers' consideration set? What would they be if your customers used your preferred cutoff criteria?
- ✓ How large a market could you persuade to use your cutoff criteria?
- ✓ Can you raise the bar on the cutoff criteria? Will that knock some competitors out of the consideration set, or will you lose some customers? Is it a favorable trade-off?
- ✓ Once you are inside the consideration set, which companies or brands are your principal competitors? Which criteria are their strengths?
- ✓ In the customer's mind, how important are your criteria? What can you do to increase the exchange rate of your criteria against those of your competitors?

Part Four

The Bottom Line

9. Busting Myths in the Marketplace Wars

In light of our understanding of the competitive playing field from earlier chapters, we can now reexamine six conventional upstream assumptions and develop new competitive strategies.

- To win against competitors, you must have the better product.
- Competitive advantage is gained by listening to customers and giving them what they want.
- You can't choose your competitors.
- Innovation means better products and technology.
- Technological improvements drive the pace and evolution of markets.
- Competitive advantage gained in the marketplace is "just marketing."

The Better Product Wins?

The first myth is that to win against competitors, you must have the better product. The assumption behind this myth appears to be that customers immediately and effortlessly switch to better products when these become available. But scratch the surface of this assumption, and you come up with more questions than winning answers. What does it mean for a product to be better? Better in what way? On what criterion or criteria? Better for whom? How do customers know or find out about better products?

Competition for the customer's mind is not won simply by demonstrating that you have a better product. It is won by increasing the importance of your criterion in consumers' evaluation, comparison, and choice of product and by associating your brand strongly with that criterion—so strongly that the brand becomes synonymous with the criterion.

Consider these observations: a BMW is about as safe as a Volvo, and a Volvo's driving dynamics are not that far off from those of a BMW. Neither brand claims it has the overall better product. Yet in customers' minds, the two brands are associated with very different characteristics, with different criteria of purchase. Volvo has always been strongly associated with safety, while BMW has always emphasized the joy of driving and holds a more "exciting" positioning. And because of their emphasis on different criteria of purchase, they appeal to very different customers. A large global study conducted by one of the two car companies aimed to find out what "excitement" meant to customers. One question asked respondents to "describe the most exciting day of your life." When the results were tallied, it turned out that BMW owners described exciting things they had done—white-water rafting in Colorado, bungee jumping in New Zealand, attending a Rolling Stones concert or a Wimbledon tournament match. In contrast, the most exciting day, by far, in the life of Volvo owners was the birth of their first child.

Positioning their brand on different criteria of purchase means that these two brands hardly compete; neither has to demonstrate that its product is superior to the other, because they aren't really competing for the same customers or promising the same benefits. Because of the criteria on which they position themselves and are so strongly associated with, the two brands attract very different types of customers, who seek very different things from their cars.

To the extent that the two brands do compete, it is to increase the importance of their respective criteria, namely, safety or the joy of driving, in the customer's consideration and purchase. The more customers use safety as a principal criterion in their purchase of a car, the more Volvo wins; the more they value the driving experience, the more BMW wins. Competition, then, is about influencing customers' criteria of purchase, about making your criteria more relevant and important to the customer, and about associating your brand closely with those criteria. It is not about demonstrating product superiority on every dimension.

This is not to say that the upstream activities of building safer cars or cars that are fun to drive do not matter. The product remains an essential ingredient in demonstrating the brand's positioning on its chosen criterion. The product and product features turn the abstract and intangible promises of the brand into real benefits for the customer. Volvo's product innovations help it remain credible on the safety criterion. The technological capabilities of building safer cars support the strategic imperative of building a lasting brand association with safety. But the product does not occupy a privileged position in the marketing mix: it is no more essential than, say, the right communication or distribution. In an organization whose center of gravity has tilted downstream, products, just as much as your other upstream and downstream activities, exist to deliver on the promises your brand makes. Intel's chips are indeed pretty fast, Volvo's cars are designed with safety in mind, and, from my interactions with them, I have found that BMW executives and engineers are remarkably obsessive about the driving experience engineered into their cars. But the products do not have to be the best on every criterion. A Toyota Prius does not have to be gorgeous; it just has to be environmentally friendly.

Listening to Customers?

The second myth is that being market oriented is a competitive advantage. A company is market oriented, according to the technical definition, if it has mastered a sequence of activities that starts with listening to customers, understanding their needs, and then developing products and services that meet those needs. Captivated by this myth, companies spend billions of dollars and countless hours conducting focus groups and surveys to understand what customers want and evaluating their reactions to product and feature prototypes. Products, prices, packaging, store placement, promotions, and positioning are pretested, then tweaked to be responsive to the "voice of the customer."

But the myth is dented when you find companies that are successful not by being responsive to customers' stated preferences but by leading customer desires. It is by now legend that when asked about the market research that went into the development of the iPad, Steve Jobs replied, "None. It's not the consumer's job to know what they want." And even when consumers know what they want, asking them may not be the best way to find out. Zara, the fast-fashion retailer does not conduct surveys to find out what customers want—it places a small unit count of products on the shelf. If the products fly off the shelf, the company quickly makes more; if not, it rapidly moves on to the next product. Downstream competitive advantage, successful companies that tilt understand, is built by influencing customer criteria of purchase and, in many cases, creating them.

At Apple's launch of the first iPhone, Jobs famously put up a picture of four smartphones that were then dominant: the Moto Q, a BlackBerry, the Palm Treo, and a Nokia E 62. In retrospect, the lineup looks like the target list for a hit job—none of those phones survived the launch of the iPhone for very long, and neither did some of the companies behind them. In his speech, Jobs explained what those phones had in common: a keyboard that took up half the usable space on the front of the phone. He denigrated the design as a very poor interface for a supposedly "smart" phone. He was craftily introducing an entirely new criterion of purchase that was to become the dominant dimension for smartphone buyers over the next five years: the touch screen that offered an infinitely flexible input interface and understood natural human gestures. At the launch, Jobs predicted that the iPhone was five years ahead of its time. None of the competitors whose phones were lined up on the screen realized then that it would take at least that long for a competitor capable of challenging the iPhone to emerge and that when one finally did, it would not come from one of the players on the screen. The reaction of the dominant incumbent in the smartphone market was typical: "It's kind of one more entrant into an already very busy space with lots of choice for consumers . . . But in terms of a sort of a sea-change for BlackBerry, I would think that's overstating it," said Jim Balsillie, then CEO of the BlackBerry maker. Later, he elaborated: "there's a lot of market research in what we do, we had a lot of market research from our customers in the markets on what the market expects from a solution . . . I am not really [one] to play a gamesmanship, my input [mechanism is] funkier than your input mechanism."[1] Indeed.

Apple had not asked customers if they wanted or preferred a touch-screen device. Apple's entry point into a crowded smartphone field was to create consumer preference for the touch screen, turn the screen interface into the primary criterion of purchase, and force competitors to follow or be left behind. But there was a catch: those that followed were seen, inevitably, as followers. It's not the customers' job to know which criteria they would like you to define; it's yours.

The importance of defining customer criteria and owning them is underscored by another lesson that often gets overlooked in the iPhone story. Despite Apple's huge success in North America, the story is different in the largest smartphone market in the world. Samsung beat the iPhone to all of the new criteria of purchase (the touch screen, the gesture control) by over a year in China. The iPhone is a challenger, not a first mover there. It was introduced late, in October 2009, and remained officially unavailable on China Mobile, the largest phone carrier, even through early 2013 (although a launch appears imminent as of this writing).[2] Samsung has defined the customer criteria in the smartphone category in China. Consequently, Apple's iPhone remains a distant sixth in the market, with a market share of less than 7 percent compared with Samsung's 24.5 percent. And as of this writing, the gap is growing.[3]

Much is made of the exhortation to managers to "change the rules of the game." But ask a dozen managers what the phrase means, and you will get at least a dozen different answers. Does it mean you should try to outdo incumbent competitors on criteria they have established (as the K-6 and PowerPC chips attempted to do by beating Intel on speed)? Or is it a reminder that you have the power to change the criteria on the playing field? It is surprising how many companies have difficulty looking beyond the former suggestion.

One reason a firm falls into the trap of attempting to outdo incumbent competitors on their well-established criteria, rather than changing the customers' criteria, is that when its market research says that customers value criteria A and B, the company assumes those criteria are fixed. Under this assumption, customers are rational actors who use all of the information at their disposal to find the best products on predetermined, unchangeable criteria. Therefore, it makes sense, in this view, to ask the customers what they want, and then it is a simple matter of giving it to them. This simply is another way of saying that when offered a better mousetrap, customers will beat a path to your door. But what customers consider a better product depends on many psychological factors, many of which are influenced by the seller. Consumer preferences are neither fixed nor given.

Which product is "better" depends, of course, on the criteria of the consumers. And you play a significant role in defining the criteria that consumers use to evaluate products. If there is one strategic lesson from competitive battles that play out over decades, it is that customers' criteria are malleable. Over time, not only can you change your position on the criteria, but you can also redraw and redefine the internal boundaries of the playing field on which you compete. This lesson applies as much to firms developing new markets (as we saw with Viagra) as it does to firms challenging entrenched incumbents in existing ones (as both Cialis and the iPhone have demonstrated).

Conventional wisdom holds that market-oriented firms tend to perform better than less-market-oriented ones, because the former uncover what consumers need and want, and align their resources to deliver just that. Instead, we've seen that customers' criteria are not inert, preexisting truths waiting to be uncovered by market-oriented firms, but rather that market-oriented firms shape consumer preferences. Successful firms don't just deliver what customers want; they determine what customers want. In the classic debate about whether marketing serves existing consumer wants or creates them, I propose that firms that do the latter build lasting competitive advantage. As a direct corollary, conventional wisdom holds that staying ahead of the game means being first to recognize and serve customer needs. The observations in this book suggest that staying ahead of competition means being first to actively define customer needs and criteria of purchase and to constantly update them.

You Can't Choose Your Competitors?

A common assumption among managers is that just as you cannot choose your relatives, you are stuck with the competitors you have. But I suggest that you can make at least three critical decisions that can determine or at least influence who you play against. First, your choice of criteria determines your competitive set. Second, your emphasis on comparison versus independent positioning influences who you compete with. And finally, your pricing places you in a competitive set.

Consider Quidel, a San Diego–based company that held nearly an 80 percent share of the medical market, but only 18 percent of the consumer market, for pregnancy testing kits. Competition was heating up as the market matured and the technology curve flattened out and most competitors offered equally accurate test kits. Quidel decided it wanted a greater share of the consumer market. To conquer the end-user market, Quidel could have taken its medical story of efficacy, accuracy, and speed to the consumer. You can picture the TV commercial: (cue baritone) "Eighty percent of doctors prefer the definitive results of Quidel's test kits." But the company chose a different tack: to ask the seemingly obvious question "Why do consumers buy pregnancy kits?"

The answer, it turned out, was not so obvious after all. There are two very different kinds of people who buy pregnancy kits: those who hopefully await a positive result and those who anxiously wish for a negative one. These two segments, Quidel reasoned, deserved to be served differently. In response, Quidel developed two offerings: one for "the hopefuls" and another for "the fearfuls." The products were differentiated in name, packaging, pricing, and in-store placement. For the fearful segment, the product was named RapidVue. It came in a plain white clinical pack design, was priced at $6.99, and was displayed near the condoms in the contraception aisle. For the hopeful segment, on the other hand, the company created a pretty pink box labeled Babystart, featuring a picture of gurgling, rosy-cheeked infant. The box was priced almost 43 percent higher, at $9.99, and was sold near the ovulation predictor kits. The segmented strategy meant that the company's consumer test kits competed in a very different consideration set, depending on which criteria of purchase was targeted. Quidel had changed who it competed with by addressing the basic question of why its customers were buying its products.[4]

Similarly, if you're in the beverage business and you've developed a rehydrating drink, you have a choice of how to position it: as a convalescence drink for digestive ailments, as a halftime drink for sports rehydration, or as a hangover reliever. In each instance, the product remains the same but the criteria customers use are different, and so are the competitors you encounter. In choosing how to position the product, managers tend to pay attention to the size and growth of the market, but neglect the intensity and identity of the competition. If you don't want to be up against giants such as Coca-Cola and Pepsi, you can choose a market with smaller competitors.

How you communicate your positioning on the criteria you've chosen will also influence who you compete with. If there are competitors you would rather be compared to, then by all means compare your brand with theirs in your communication, place your product next to theirs on the shelf, buy distribution space that emphasizes the comparison, and develop comparable pack sizes and formats. Brita, the water filter brand, ensures shelf positioning next to bottled waters in the grocery store, in addition to its position in the housewares aisle. The purpose is to enter the bottled-water consideration set and encourage consumers to compare Brita with the Evian and Dasani bottled water brands. In the bottled-water aisle, the placement of Brita presents consumers with criteria such as the per-gallon price of clean water and the environmentally friendly option of not having to discard plastic water bottles. On both criteria, Brita has the advantage.

On the other hand, of course, if you would prefer not to be compared with other brands, then you're better off communicating, distributing, and packaging your products so that they are less comparable. Yet, a trip to the grocery store and a glance at online catalogs show how similar product packaging is. (Why are all yogurts sold in the same pack size and format, and why is the communication of brands so indistinguishable that consumers cannot recall the brand after having seen the advertisement?) The lack of differentiation encourages competition, when many of these brands would be better off avoiding it.

Finally, pricing will place your product within or outside the consideration set and has a strong influence on who you compete with. When Infiniti launched its comeback car, the G35, in the early part of this century, the vehicle was hailed as a BMW-beater. Loosely based on the legendary Nissan Skyline (and sold under the Skyline brand in Japan), the car had interior room and engine power comparable to a BMW 5 Series. But the car would have struggled to compete with the 5 Series for a number of reasons. First, the 5 Series is not an entry-level BMW, so it is aimed at experienced buyers of BMWs or at least buyers who have previously owned a luxury automobile. Moreover, the 5 Series is an expensive car, and when a customer is shelling out that kind of money, he or she is not looking for value, but is looking for an established brand and an established value proposition. So it made sense for Infiniti to position the G35 against the BMW 3 Series. Pricing accomplished that objective. Car consumers, it turns out, use price as a cutoff criterion in forming their consideration set. And so do journalists covering the automobile market. Because the G35 was priced close to the BMW 3 Series, coverage of its launch placed it in tests against the 3 Series rather than the 5 Series.

Choosing to avoid competitors may minimize head-on competition, but there is no guarantee that competitors will not follow. You may still have to contend with competitors you did not want or ask for. But chances are that competitors will be deterred from following you because of the low payoff of a me-too strategy. And if you have done your homework and established dominance on your criterion of purchase, they will be placing themselves in an unfavorable competitive position unless they bear the cost of building their own criteria.

Counterintuitively, you have more say in determining who your competitors are if you are a later entrant in a marketplace than if you are a first entrant. A later entrant can choose to compete directly with an incumbent or to differentiate. An incumbent is subject to the decisions of later entrants. But an incumbent is not helpless: it stays ahead of competitors by continually redefining the market, introducing new criteria of purchase, and slicing existing ones more finely.

Is Innovation Merely Better Products and Technology?

A persistent myth that innovation is about better products and technologies leads managers to an overreliance on products to win competitive battles. Two aspects of downstream reasoning undermine this myth. First, as we have seen in several case examples, it is a marketer's influence over customers' criteria of purchase—and not better products—that delivers competitive wins. Second, a company wins competitive battles by offering the customer better downstream value. Value is increasingly the result of reducing customers' costs and risks over the entire purchase, consumption, and disposal cycle. Innovation, for companies that tilt, is about creating new forms of value for customers and finding new ways to reduce their costs and risks.

In pitched battle, when one player switches to this broader definition of innovation, competitors are caught by surprise. In previous chapters, we have seen how ICI's shift from selling explosives to selling contracts for broken rock changed the value proposition for customers and altered the game for competitors. We also saw how by offering vendor-managed inventory, MasterBuilders reduced its customers' risk of a stock-out and left competitors scrambling. Several other examples in the book also showed how tilting innovation to the downstream delivered more value for customers without the need to build better products.

Technology as the Driver of Innovation?

Changes in technology are sometimes thought to be the greatest threat to competitive advantage. But the changes are only relevant if they upend downstream competitive advantage. You don't need to sweat every product launch, every new feature introduction by a competitor—just pay attention to those that attempt to wrest control of the customers' criteria of purchase. It was not the advent of digital photography, or Kodak's shortcomings in that technology that ultimately shuttered the company—it was Kodak's failure to update its brand associations to shifting criteria of purchase.

After more than a century of blade technology, Gillette still controls when the market moves on to the next generation of razor and blade. And even though for the past three decades, competitors have known that the next-generation blade from Gillette will carry one additional cutting edge and some added swivel or vibration, they've never preempted the third, fourth, or fifth blade. Why? Because there is little to gain from preemption. Gillette owns the customers' criterion, and the additional blade becomes credible and viable only when Gillette decides to introduce it, backed by a billion-dollar launch campaign. In other words, Gillette owns the dimension on which shaving innovation is defined in the consumers' mind: four blades are better than three, but only if Gillette says so. Its advantage resides downstream. It sets the pace of change in the industry because of its clout in determining when consumers switch. Technological improvements don't drive the pace and evolution in this market; marketing does. Technology is an enabler.

Markets are characterized by evolutionary, generational, and revolutionary changes, all of which can be understood in terms of mechanisms of consumer psychology. *Evolutionary changes* push the boundaries of existing criteria of purchase: higher horsepower or fuel efficiency for cars, higher processing speeds for semiconductor chips, ever more cutting edges on a Gillette blade, higher-potency pills. *Generational changes* introduce new criteria that complement old ones and open new market segments: sugar-free chewing gum and soft drinks, hybrid vehicles, pull-up diapers, once-a-day pills where multiple pills were required. *Revolutionary changes* not only introduce new criteria, but also render old ones obsolete: the new video-game controllers from Nintendo Wii changed how gamers interact with their games, rendering older interfaces obsolete; touch screens and multitouch interfaces in smartphones changed what customers expect from a smartphone and made the pre-touch-screen phones obsolete; a vaccine for tuberculosis, AIDS, or malaria would make current treatments for these diseases almost redundant within a couple of decades.

The market power required to move the market increases as you move from evolutionary to generational to revolutionary change. In each case, the quality of the product innovation and the increased benefits relative to current products help move the market, but do not guarantee that it will move. Both AMD's K-6 chip and the PowerPC chip were faster than the fastest Intel chip on the market at the time of their launch. But the two challengers were unable to move the market.

Technology is a necessary but insufficient condition in the evolution of markets. New products offer no guarantee of success. Marketing offers the mechanism for moving customers through evolutionary, generational, and revolutionary changes. It does this by reducing the risk of new-product introductions and of perpetuating a successful product. Market success is founded on the introduction of new criteria into the customers' purchase vocabulary and consumption scripts.

Just Marketing?

Conventional wisdom dismisses the competitive advantage gained in the marketplace as "just marketing." Critics of marketing advantage argue that it is somehow not real or lasting, because it relies on consumer impressions, or that it is not sustainable, because competitors can make the same claims. Compared with advantage from other sources, such as innovation (R&D laboratories) and better products (manufacturing superiority), competitive advantage gained through marketing is thought to be weak. Some of this contempt for downstream advantage is justly traceable to marketing practices that add little value, attempts by marketers to sell snake oil, and a track record of selling Pet Rocks. But the previous chapters' examples help dispel this myth by demonstrating the lasting advantage that organizations that tilt can create in the marketplace by systematically addressing customers' costs and risks. In the next chapter, we examine what makes downstream advantage durable and sustainable.

The Myths Checklist

✓ Do you compete by trying to demonstrate to customers that you have the better product? In the customers' mind, are the dimensions on which you demonstrate "better" owned by you or your competitors?

✓ Is a portion of your marketing budget consumed trying to ascertain whether consumers like your products? Do you spend time and money worrying about how consumers will react to every little change in product, distribution, price, and communication? Can you redirect those resources toward determining the criteria that are important to customers, understanding why they buy, and learning why some consumers don't buy from you?

✓ How do you choose your competitors? How do you determine who your competitors are and what you can do to avoid them?

✓ Are planning meetings and watercooler conversations in your company about new products? How can you redirect these conversations and resources toward customer criteria of purchase?

✓ Do your marketing department and sales force count on new products to ease competitive pressures? Which innovative initiatives from these departments have contributed to customer value and to gaining control of customer criteria of purchase?

✓ Does the marketing department garner respect in your company, or is it regarded as a cost center? Do other functions wonder how the marketing department adds value? Are marketing's contributions trivialized? Are they considered insufficiently strategic?

10. Understanding Why Downstream Competitive Advantage Is Sustainable

Before you tilt your business and invest in your downstream activities and innovation, you want to know that any advantage you capture there is sustainable. In this chapter, I will try to address that question, as well as another: what makes downstream competitive advantage more sustainable than your classic garden-variety upstream competitive advantage? So far, we've had glimpses of the sustainability of the downstream strategies that companies adopt. We saw how competitors are unable to respond because they have not built up a big picture and how difficult it is to secure the data to build a big picture if you're a later entrant. We saw how brands build lasting associations with primary criteria of purchase and how Intel turned its brand into a criterion of purchase, giving itself a downstream advantage that competitors with faster chips were unable to dislodge. In this chapter, we look at the fundamental reasons why these strategies confer enduring advantage. I adopt two approaches to answer the question. First, I examine what the successful strategies have in common, and second, I look to research in economics and consumer psychology. The short answer is that downstream competitive advantage is more sustainable for the following reasons:

- It has network effects, its locus is distributed, it resides in the marketplace, and it yields insights that are unique.
- Cognitive inertia means that customers favor incumbent brands, giving these brands an advantage. Inertia, the tendency for consumers to stick with what they know, is due to several factors, including the momentum of dominant brands, customers' confirmatory biases, the prevalence of prior beliefs, loss aversion (a consumer preference for what a person already possesses), and habit.

Let's unpack each of these.

Network Effects

You will not find Facebook's competitive advantage locked up somewhere in its sparkling new offices at Menlo Park or even roaming free on the premises. The company that has gone from dorm room to $6 billion in revenue in less than a decade still counts fewer than five thousand employees. The employees are smart and very productive, but they are not its most irreplaceable asset. If you're thinking it is the one billion users who have accounts on the website, you're much closer. But what is it about those users that makes them such an advantage? The key for Facebook, it turns out, is in something called *network effects*. For those who want to be a part of a social network, it makes sense to congregate where everybody else is hanging out. There is only one village square on the Internet, and it is run by Facebook. Being on a different square from everyone else doesn't get you anywhere—you just miss the party. In other words, the need of Facebook users to be where everyone else is constitutes the social network's key advantage. Facebook does everything possible to keep it that way and to avoid the mistakes of earlier social networks such as MySpace, which came close to building network effects and then lost them as the party moved elsewhere. The data that users post on Facebook is not portable to any other site;

the time lines, the connections, the events, the gaming partners, and the apps create stickiness, so users don't leave. And the more the users stay, the more their friends are likely to stay.

Network effects are a classic downstream competitive advantage. They reside in the marketplace, are distributed (you can't point to a network effect—it resides in the rationale for connections among consumers), and are difficult to replicate. From that advantage flows another critical downstream advantage for Facebook: it has the largest and most detailed database on the preferences, habits, and surfing and consuming behavior of the largest number of customers ever to have been assembled. The company monetizes this data by selling advertisers access to its users. And the data, too, is subject to a positive feedback loop that Facebook ignited: the more information users share, the more their friends share information. Upstart competitors such as Pip.io, Altly.com, The Fridge, and Collegiate Nation and new entrants backed by awesome Internet power, such as Google+ may offer features such as greater privacy or group video chat. But they fail to create the positive feedback loop, because it makes sense for everybody to be where everybody else already is; being on Facebook reduces interaction costs and risks. Who wants to incur the costs of opening and maintaining a social network account where their friends are not? The competitive advantages of network effects and data are not just sustainable; they are accumulative: the more the company seizes competitive advantage, the greater the reason for the market to cede it more of that competitive advantage.

Curiously, brands, too, benefit from two types of network effects. The first one is obvious: "I want what others want." Watch high school kids buy products because other kids have them—Ugg boots, for example. Or think of the herd effects that make or break movies. With social networks' rapid dissemination of information, these types of brand network effects have been turbocharged—they occur more rapidly and forcefully than before. A movie now flops or hits as a result of the first forty-eight hours of tweeting and box office sales.

The second type of brand network effect is a little less obvious. Think of it this way: the reason people buy and drive a Mercedes is not that the car is more reliable, a better drive, or more cost-effective (it may or may not be any of those). The reason some customers drive a Mercedes is that others know what a Mercedes is. The Mercedes plays to a gallery, an audience that knows what the brand stands for. The members of this audience understand they're supposed to be awed by a Mercedes, even if they may never buy one themselves. Because of its signaling value, the three-point star of the brand confers status, prestige, and all the other forms of social benefit. And the more people who know what a Mercedes is, the more valuable the badge is to those doing the buying and driving.

If few people outside the target market for Mercedes knew what a Mercedes was or recognized the status and prestige it is meant to confer, would the badge still command a premium? Would as many people buy it? The loyalty and premium are the results of the network effect of the Mercedes brand. It is a formidable downstream competitive advantage.

There are two marketing implications of brand network effects, one obvious, the other less so. First, your marketing dollars get a much bigger bang for the buck if you can win over opinion leaders. Their use of your product will sell it to others as a result of the "I want what they have" network effect. Facebook's victory over MySpace can, in part, be attributed to this effect. This prescription is widely accepted and practiced by marketers—so not much new here. The second implication comes from the second type of network effect and offers the opposite prescription: don't just preach to the converted. For your brand to have value to your consumers, those not in your target market need to know about how great it is. So how do we reconcile the two opposing prescriptions?

The answer is, you have to do both. Target both those in the direct target market (those who are most likely to buy your brand) and those in the gallery. But target the two groups with very different messages. Those in your direct target market need to be brought through the entire hierarchy of effects—awareness, knowledge, liking, preference, conviction, purchase, and post purchase—so they require fine-tuned communication at every step. Those in the gallery, however, only require the first two steps (awareness and knowledge) for brand network effects to do their magic.

Remember, of course, that this type of competitive advantage is difficult for competitors to replicate, because it resides in the marketplace and is distributed—there is no single location of this competitive advantage. Its locus is in the positive feedback loops between consumers, in the invisible influence relationships between people, and in consumers' beliefs and behavior. For brands, the competitive advantage thus resides in the minds of millions of consumers and in the relationships among those consumers; for Facebook, the competitive advantage resides in the behavior of a billion users and their connections.

Cognitive Inertia

Cognitive inertia prevents easy switching across brands, giving the incumbent an advantage. In any purchase, customers seek a reasonable and satisfactory, if not optimal, outcome. They'd like their products to work, their insurance to pay out when it is needed, their bank and telecom carrier to keep their money safe and not drop their calls. People want their apparel, phone, and automobiles to make the fashion statements they want them to make, and their food to be tasty, safe, and sometimes even nutritious and healthy. To minimize the chances of a poor choice, or to make as good a choice as possible, the customer is often willing to put in some effort. He or she might search for information, learn about products and services and how to use them, and then mentally store the information. Later, the customer could retrieve the information when it is required for a choice and could compare and evaluate information about the alternatives being considered. In other words, the customer is willing to incur costs to reduce risk.

Many of the costs the customer incurs are cognitive: the costs of thinking. And by now, the tilt thesis is familiar: companies and brands that can help their customers reduce these costs, the underlying risks, or both are valued by customers, who therefore often pay a premium for these brands, are more loyal to them, and may even buy more from these brands. But how sustainable is this downstream competitive advantage? Can competitors easily replicate it? Will customers immediately switch to competitors who do?

Sustainability is the result of customers' stickiness or inertia—that is, customers' unwillingness or inability to immediately switch to a competitor when the competitor offers equivalent or better value. Millions or billions of individual choices to not switch add up to a sustainable competitive advantage, favoring the incumbent. This is not to say that challengers can never oust an incumbent or that the customer will never switch for better value. But the holder of a competitive advantage enjoys a buffer from competition—a buffer that cushions competitive shocks. It takes a long time and a lot of mistakes for a Kodak, a BlackBerry, or a Nokia to lose its customers or even its growth momentum, and incumbent brands can weather storms such as product defects, product launch delays, and product recalls and still maintain market share.

The cognitive processes that customers use to minimize their costs of information acquisition, learning, storage, retrieval, comparison, evaluation, and choice also underlie stickiness. Let's unpack these processes to see how they favor the incumbent.

The Momentum of Dominant Brands

Brands that have achieved dominance at the center of a category (Nike in athletic shoes, Coke in cola beverages, Pampers in the diapers aisle, Tide in laundry detergents, the Apple iPhone in smartphones, and Gatorade in sports drinks) attract consumers simply by being what they are because of their dominance in the category. They tend both to occupy the most meaningful and most frequently used criteria of purchase in the category and to have the dominant market share in the category. Retailers and distributors hand them lots of prime eye-level shelf space. These brands are usually the first brands that consumers learn of in the category; if consumers are aware of no other brands of cola, for example, they will have heard of Coke. And once they are aware of Coke, it will inevitably enter their consideration set. That is no accident, as not only do these brands tend to have dominant advertising budgets, but they are also the brands about which the most secondary information exists in the marketplace—people talk and write about these brands. Similar momentum effects are evident in the allocation of retail promotions, media coverage, and page rank. The dominant brand is much more likely to get prized resources, even without asking or paying for them, and when it does, consumers notice it more, paying more attention to what this brand says than to what its lesser competitors say.[1]

Over time, dominant brands consolidate this advantage by becoming the default in the category. When consumers recall brands in the category, for example, when forming a consideration set, the dominant brand's strong association with the category virtually ensures its inclusion. When you think of online video calling, Skype immediately comes to mind. Its many competitors have to work much harder to be included in the consideration set and may even be inhibited when the dominant brand is recalled. Brand recall is correlated with market share, which in turn feeds dominance in consumers' minds, increasing the probability of recall. Yes, it's another example of a classic positive feedback loop that leads to an accumulative advantage. The more you have of the competitive advantage, the more you're likely to gain more of it.

When consumers are in doubt about the brand they saw in an advertisement or in a store, they often misattribute competitors' advertising and store presence to the dominant brand. When a competitor introduces a new feature it considers an advantage, many consumers nullify that advantage by assuming the dominant brand also has the feature. The consumers' default assumption is that Kleenex is the brand they use, even when they're blowing their nose into some other brand of facial tissue. Dominant brands are able to efficiently introduce new products as brand extensions. These new products benefit from existing brand awareness, reducing the costs and risks of new-product trial for customers and significantly lowering for the seller the cost of launch relative to competitors' products.

All in all, dominant brands possess a momentum that gives them a tailwind: they have to work less for the same result that their competitors achieve (or work the same for a better payoff than their competitors). This advantage is illustrated by the advertising costs of dominant brands. They tend to spend more than their competitors on advertising in absolute terms, but less than their competitors per dollar of sales. Why? The dominant players benefit from customers' conversations in the marketplace, from customers' default assumptions about the category, from retailers' and complementors' default decisions, and even from competitors' advertising dollars.

Prior Beliefs and Confirmatory Bias

Ask any customer if he or she is persuaded or even slightly influenced by advertising, and you'll get the "no, not I" response, which is sometimes followed by a "but I know that others are" afterthought. In other words, advertising, according to customer self-reports, is a terribly ineffectual marketing tool. Even if they pay attention to ads, customers don't believe the claims, distrusting them as highly partisan sources of information issued by marketers with ulterior motives. And yet marketers continue to spend billions of dollars every year trying to persuade customers through their advertising. Either the marketers are wasting their money, or they know something customers don't. Here's what they do know: marketing expenditures correlate with sales. If you increase advertising relative to your competitors, you sell more, and if you cut advertising relative to competitors, sales volume drops. So, companies continuc to spend money on advertising, knowing that at a macro level, if not at the micro, individual-customer level, advertising does seem to spur sales.

Over the years, consumer research has shown that whether advertising does or does not directly persuade or incite customers to buy, and whether customers actually believe advertised claims or not, it has a more subtle and enduring effect that eventually gets customers to persuade themselves. Here is how it works. Exposure to an advertising claim, such as "A Lexus offers the smoothest ride," may not convince consumers that a Lexus offers the smoothest ride, but the claim does register in their minds. It primes potential customers to test the hypothesis that a Lexus may indeed offer a smooth ride. When they have an opportunity to test that hypothesis, riding in a friend's Lexus or on a test drive at the dealership, they seek evidence to confirm that the ride in a Lexus is indeed smooth. And if they find evidence consistent with their "smooth" hypothesis, they're much more likely to be convinced of the superiority of Lexus.[2]

But deconstructing this hypothesis formation and testing process shows the imperfections of the customers' conclusions. It points out the opportunities for marketers to influence customer deliberations, and highlights the source of sustainable downstream competitive advantage rooted in customer beliefs. First, the customers' hypotheses are about criteria that the marketer wants them to think about, wants to be evaluated and compared on, and wants the customers to use as key criteria in both the cutoff and the trade-off phases of decision making. If the customers use the smooth-ride criterion to evaluate cars and in so doing place a lower importance on other criteria such as fuel efficiency or price, the Lexus brand already enjoys a big win. If the use of this criterion blocks out or reduces the importance of other criteria such as fuel efficiency or German manufacture, Lexus enjoys an even bigger win.

Next, in testing the smooth-ride hypothesis, the customer looks for evidence of a smooth ride in a Lexus. The actual ride experience in a Lexus is deemed to confirm the hypothesis. Case closed. Importantly, the hypothesis attunes the customer to look for information related to the hypothesis test. Most customers do not look for disconfirmatory evidence: does a BMW or a Mercedes also offer as smooth a ride? Does a Lexus offer or not offer superior performance on criteria other than a smooth ride? Not having been primed to look for a smooth ride in competitor cars, the customer may not even pay attention to how smooth a ride these brands offer. In other words, the customer seeks sufficiency tests (does a Lexus offer a smooth ride?), not necessity tests (does it have to be a Lexus to offer a smooth ride?).

Confirmatory tests are remarkably persuasive and remarkably pervasive. Even in ambiguous product environments where the quality of a product is hard to distinguish from the quality of another, consumers are confident they can pick out the better product (the better beer, the better wine, the better paper towel, the better ketchup, the better cola etc.) through product experience. And research shows that their choices and evaluations after product experience are a function of whether the consumers were exposed to advertising ahead of time. Interestingly, when measured immediately after exposure to advertising, their evaluations show no differences—brands whose ads the consumers have seen are not evaluated better than brands whose ads they have not seen. But once the consumers have a chance to test their hypothesis through product trial, the hypothesis planted in their mind by advertising evidently shapes their experience with the product, and they favor the product for which they have seen an ad. One reason the one-two punch of advertising exposure and product trial may be so persuasive is that the customer knows (or believes) he or she is in control of the testing environment. Control over what is tested, how it is tested, how the evidence is interpreted, and the consumer's own conclusions combine to give the person tremendous confidence in his or her judgments. Consumers persuade themselves.

The confirmatory bias is not limited to interpretation of advertising information. Preferred brands also benefit from a favorable reception for their brand extensions and receive the benefit of the doubt when products fail or have to be recalled because they are defective or dangerous. The search for confirmatory evidence also implies that customers ignore disconfirmatory evidence. For example, as we saw earlier, customers who are convinced of the superiority of German-engineered cars ignore third-party test information about the relative inferiority of these cars on dimensions such as driving dynamics and reliability.[3]

The confirmatory bias enhances incumbency advantages because customers' prior beliefs are strongest for brands they possess or buy on a regular basis. Their interpretation of marketplace information occurs in the context of those prior beliefs. And prior beliefs are notoriously difficult to change. The confirmatory bias is perhaps most potent after purchase. Customers who have committed to a brand by buying it seek evidence that they made a sound decision. Information in the environment related to this pops out at them. A new car buyer is surprised by how many others made the same choice—the buyer notices the selected brand of car much more than if he or she had not bought the car. This is a sign that the buyer is seeking out confirmatory evidence to justify the choice. Positive information is sought out more than negative information. The more a person does this, the more he or she is satisfied with the choice, and the less the person is collecting favorable information about other brands, consolidating the incumbent's advantage.

Recent research in psychology suggests that the confirmatory bias is so pervasive because it is hardwired into human thinking. This explanation suggests that *thinking* is in fact persuasion and itself is inherently a social act: thinking is anticipation about "how do I persuade others?" So if we're thinking in order to persuade, we are actually marshaling evidence to support our arguments and neglecting arguments that don't. In other words, when we evaluate a hypothesis picked from an advertisement, the habit of conducting sufficiency tests rather than necessity tests is so fundamental that, despite its flaws, we would have difficulty thinking in any other way.[4]

Loss Aversion and the Endowment Effect

Customers like what they have and are averse to losing it. Studies in behavioral economics have repeatedly shown that people on average must be paid twice as much to give up something that they possess than they would pay to acquire the same thing. In one experiment, for example, subjects randomly assigned to receive a mug put an average price of $7.12 on it when asked to sell the mug. Subjects randomly assigned as buyers in the same experiment said they would, on average, pay no more than $2.87 to acquire the same mug. Economic utility, it appears, is subject to changes in state (the perceived loss of going from having to not having), not just from the state of possessing an object. Customers tend to be biased toward the status quo and prefer not to trade it off for something new or different. The longer that customers have owned an object, the more averse they are to losing it: they value it more and they find it more attractive. This *endowment effect*, as it is known, not only applies to objects, but has also been suggested as one explanation for brand loyalty. In other words, brands that have no other advantage than that they are already in the hands of customers can count on some measure of inertia because customers are averse to switching.[5] This aversion to loss sustains inertia, to the incumbent's advantage.

Habit

A customer regularly buys a bottle of Evian water from the vending machine at the gym after a workout. For many low-cost, low-involvement, frequently purchased, and highly familiar products, customers develop routines that allow them to minimize the cognitive effort (cost of thinking) required in deciding which brand to buy, how to buy it, how to use it, and how to dispose of it. The routine dictates the occasion, the location, and the brand, and ensures that the consumption behavior can be executed without thought—without the intermediate steps of consideration set formation and selection from the set. Habitual scripts unfurl, rather than occur. The customer's routine is a significant advantage for the Evian brand over competitors: the brand no longer needs to spend time, effort, and money persuading the customer to buy. It just needs to do everything possible to keep the cost of the customer's decision making low by buying exclusivity at the vending location, ensuring the product is always in stock so that the customer is not forced out of his or her habitual behavior, and packaging the product in its familiar plastic bottles and colors so that it is easily recognized without cognitive effort. And then it needs to get out of the way, as habit takes over. Once that happens, competitors are not just competing against the power of the Evian brand and consumer preference for it; they are competing against the force of consumer habit, which is very difficult to break.

In summary, companies gain competitive advantage by tilting their center of gravity downstream. The competitive advantage resides in the marketplace. It resides in the networks in the market, in the relationships between sellers and buyer, in the connections between customers, and in the networks that reside in the customers' minds. Its effects are evident in the nature of competition, customer behavior, market shares, and profits.

The Sustainability Checklist

✓ Does your product or brand benefit from network effects? How can you foster network effects?

✓ What hypotheses about your brand or product do you set up for consumers to test?

✓ What confirmatory information do you provide consumers before and during their test of the hypothesis?

✓ How do you saturate the purchase and consumption environment with confirmatory evidence?

✓ What type of post-purchase information do you provide that confirms the customers' choice?

✓ How do you confirm and validate the value that the customers attach to your product or brand once they own it?

✓ How do you build your product or brand into a consumption routine? What do you do to facilitate the customers' routine?

11. Tilting Your Strategy and Organization

A downstream tilt leaves industries and the companies that play in them altered forever. As costs, value creation, and sources of competitive advantage tilt downstream, industry landscapes are overhauled: new forms of value are created, companies that seize new forms of advantage thrive, and those that don't scurry for survival or lag. For firms, the tilt implies change on multiple fronts, notably, changes in strategy formulation, the way firms are organized, downstream functions such as marketing and sales, and competition in global marketplaces. The changes are deep, widespread, and, for businesses with large upstream investments and a commitment to managing for the upstream, often difficult.

For over 250 years, sourcing, manufacturing, logistics, and technological progress have been at the center of business activity. All other business activities grew around this core. Strategically, business has honed skills to spot and capture upstream sources of competitive advantage, notably, scale and product innovation. Organizationally, companies are invested in systems that keep the upstream machine humming, processes that maximize throughput, and trained managers who worship the gods of efficiency. By now, your business knows what it takes to make and move stuff. The problem is, so does everybody else.

Still, many businesses are run as though the major fixed costs, the primary customer value, and the key competitive advantages reside in the upstream. These businesses continue to emphasize volume throughput and upstream efficiency. They think of product innovation as their key to a brighter future, often to the detriment of a customer focus, a broadened understanding of customer needs, economies of scope, downstream innovation, cost and risk reduction, and ownership of the criteria of purchase. Whether in response to shifting competitive pressures within the industry or to preemptively capture a first-mover advantage in your industry, if you're considering tilting your business, this chapter describes what it will take.

Implications for Strategy

The tilt to downstream competitive advantage carries three implications that go to the heart of strategy. First, its locus is no longer within the firm, but resides increasingly downstream, in the marketplace, in interactions with customers. Second, firms have an opportunity to aim for more than merely *sustainable* competitive advantage; they can build *accumulative* competitive advantage. And third, the skills and resources required to make and move stuff can be bought or brought in, while those required to connect and engage with customers need to be owned and honed.

A CEO faces the task of steering his or her firm to generate returns that are above those achieved by competing firms. Whether the firm is a start-up looking to grow its business or a large company in a mature industry looking to extricate itself from bruising competition, it has traditionally sought advantage in better products or better ways of making and moving those products. In some industries, more-progressive firms have relied on softer forms of competitive advantage, such as people, proprietary processes (e.g., a streamlined ability to churn out new products, or a glass company's patented processes to develop ultrathin silicon wafers for the semiconductor or solar panel industries), or unique knowledge (e.g., an oil company's ability to find and develop oil fields). Each of these sources of competitive advantage carries the alluring possibility of shelter from competitors, provided, of course, that the advantage can be kept from competitors. But there is a catch: many of these advantages, or their end products, are now available for purchase on the open market. Better products can be designed and manufactured for you by third-party specialists—the same specialists who make stuff for your competitors. What's more, the efficiency and quality benefits of proprietary processes and knowledge are baked into the low costs of sourcing from specialist producers—for you, as well as for your competitors.

The tilt strategy urges the CEO to seek competitive advantage in the firm's interactions with the marketplace, in the networks with and between customers, and on the playing field inside the customers' mind. By asking fundamental questions such as "Why do our customers buy from us?" the firm brings the voice of the customer into strategy formulation. Uncovering the reasons why shows that the customers buy from the firm (rather than from its competitors) because it helps reduce their costs and risks. The CEO should be busy (1) seeking out more customers who value a similar reduction in costs and risks and (2) uncovering additional costs and risks that the firm can reduce for its existing customers.

A second implication for strategy is that you should expect more from your competitive advantage than you have become accustomed to. The best that strategists expect from their competitive advantage is that it will be sustainable—that is, they expect that for a reasonable period, competitors will be unable to copy it. The reasonable period could be a year or two in a fast-moving industry or a decade or two in a slower-moving one. But the expectation is that over time, the gap closes. Competitors catch up, technological change neutralizes your advantage, regulation or deregulation throws a wrench in the works, or disruptive start-ups find new ways of doing the same thing more cheaply. Eventually, however, even the most optimistic strategist expects even the most sustainable competitive advantage to erode. Competitive advantage is thought to have a half-life.

Of course, you might point out, competitive advantage has always had more going for it than mere sustainability. It has always had *momentum*. The very fact of having a competitive advantage, particularly one that is widely known through the brand, attracts additional advantages. Google finds it easier to recruit better people than, say, Yahoo! does, because Google has a reputation as a leader in its field. Suppliers quote lower prices to BMW than to competitors, simply for the privilege (and, presumably, the bragging rights) of doing business with it. Momentum means that the company's competitive advantage solidifies over time and wanes more slowly in the face of competition or the firm's own mistakes and mismanagement. Momentum means that advantage is the company's to lose.

But several of the case examples we have examined in the preceding chapters suggest a type of competitive advantage that goes even farther, beyond momentum: it is *accumulative* and accelerates over time and with experience. ICI's ability to accumulate data on quarry blasts and to use it to create more efficient blasts for customers gives the company an advantage in gathering even more data from customers' blasts. The more ICI has an advantage in persuading customers to share their blast data, the less its competitors have access to the data. The gap between holder for that type of competitive advantage and its competitors grows rather than shrinks over time. Similarly, as we saw in chapter 10, Facebook users share their data with the company because other users do. Network effects in data sharing mean that Facebook benefits from positive feedback loops in the uploading of user information, and competitors do not. Witness the difficulty that Google+, a Facebook competitor, had in getting off the ground. Despite a high initial user sign-up rate and the significant backing of Google, users were simply not uploading as much information to the site as they were on Facebook. The challenger's task is made even more difficult in the face of accumulative advantages because it not only has to close the gap with the leader that exists today, but must also close the additional distance that the leader will have covered by the time today's gap is closed.

Organizing to Deliver Downstream Value

A downstream tilt also entails several changes in the way firms are organized to deliver value. The first, and most telling, aspect of a downstream organization is the focus of management attention. Return to the question that opened this book: when you ask managers what business they are in, do they respond with a description of the product or means of production, or do they talk about their customers, the customer benefits they deliver, and their downstream advantage? In upstream-focused organizations, conversations and meetings dwell on products and aspects of production that managers believe distinguish them from competitors.

In downstream-focused organizations, the problems that preoccupy managers are about acquiring, satisfying, and retaining customers; about reducing costs and risks for customers; and about managing information that flows through the networks that connect the organization to its customers, and customers to each other; and about criteria of purchase. Importantly, these activities are not left to the marketing or sales departments, but pervade the organization. The downstream is too important to be left to the marketing and sales folks alone.

Cross-functional teams huddle to innovate the firm's downstream activities: to develop systems to reduce customers' costs and risks at each stage of interaction. The firm allocates budgets for the acquisition, retention, and satisfaction of customers, but it also invests in building platforms that will make these activities more efficient for both the firm and the customer. Since managers manage what is measured, the tilted business uses yardsticks that focus on the market. Customer funnels, the costs of serving a customer, the costs of retaining one, the costs and risks that customers incur in doing business with the firm, the lifetime value and profitability of each customer, customer churn, revenue per user, and share of wallet form the basis for management discussions of strategy and tactics, and metrics of success.

The planning horizons in upstream firms are limited. As chapter 1 explained, the strategic question that drives upstream-focused firms is "How much more of this stuff can we make and sell?" Organizationally, this often translates into a planning horizon that is tied to the life cycles of products. Resources are allocated to products according to their life cycle stage, with the strategic goal of maximizing volume throughput during the finite life cycle. A portfolio of products helps balance overall corporate performance by blending the ups and downs of multiple life cycles. Product teams may attempt to extend the life cycles of their products through product innovation and pricing, but despite their best efforts, the horizon remains finite: everyone knows the product's life will eventually come to an end, either because it will be superseded by other products within the product category or because the entire category will be rendered obsolete by another.

Downstream firms, in contrast, are driven by a different strategic question: "What else do my customers want?" Inherent in this question is the implication that the company's core competence resides in its ability to understand customer needs and to do whatever it takes to fulfill them, even if the needs stray from the products the company currently makes and sells. In other words, strategy is anchored on customer needs, rather than on the firm's products or production facilities. Such a strategy is more flexible by design: it follows evolving customer needs. If the needs stray from the current product portfolio, the company will find the resources to deliver for those changed needs. Organizationally, this means recognizing that a company cannot do everything: contracting with outside suppliers is common, and the formation of alliances is critical. A downstream firm sees itself at the nexus between a range of possible suppliers on the one hand and the customer segments that it knows intimately and that trust the company to deliver value on the other.

The planning horizons of downstream firms are tied to market segments (a group of customers who have the same need and buy using similar criteria of purchase) rather than to products, and hence look out to infinity. As segments shift or as their needs evolve or are fulfilled differently, the company adapts. Note the similarity of this ideal with what Ted Levitt envisioned fifty years ago: railway companies that see themselves as fulfilling transportation needs rather than as being in the railroad business are more likely to be flexible and less dogmatic about how those transportation needs are fulfilled. They are not bound to their physical track and rolling-stock infrastructure; nor do they see rail as the only means of fulfilling customer needs. If a focus on customer needs sometimes means jettisoning legacy products, outsourcing production, moving into new industries, and mergers and acquisitions, as necessary, to serve the customers, then firms should be prepared to do so. Apple, after all, was an outsider to both the music industry and the telephone handset industry. It established a position in both industries because it saw that customers could be better served than they were by existing companies.

Product innovation, a mainstay of competitive advantage for the upstream-focused firm, is not immune to the downstream tilt. In the downstream, product innovation, like production, is subservient to the primary source of competitive advantage—the customers' needs—and consequently must respond to very strict criteria of flexibility and usability. These criteria may be better met when innovation itself is contracted out rather than run in-house.

Silicon Valley exemplifies a model of outsourced product innovation that, counterintuitively, speaks to the importance of the downstream. Large, well-established firms in Silicon Valley focus on building markets and connections to customers, while outsourcing R&D and product development to smaller, nimbler firms. Sometimes, the venture-capital arms of the larger firms take a stake in these smaller firms, but often, the larger firms leave this risk to third-party investors. They only step in when the start-up has proved its concept or, better still, proved that it can generate revenue. Then they may take a stake in the start-up as a means of locking up the technology or acquire the entire firm so as to scale it to their market. Alternatively, large firms may simply license-in the start-up's technology, knowing that regardless of which party owns the technology, they have a hold on market access. This model of outsourced product innovation is gaining ground in other industries as well, following a downstream tilt. Examples include pharmaceuticals and even consumer goods and automobiles.[1]

Unsurprisingly, downstream-focused firms are not wedded to their technology. As technological cycles come and go, customer needs remain these firms' defining axis. The firms are able to weather technological shifts better than upstream-focused firms. Had it followed a downstream tilt, Kodak might still have been in business if it had leveraged its brand to move consumers to digital technology, rather than attempted to use its brand to slow the shift. Similarly, Sony would have been delivering consumer entertainment over the cloud a decade ago, and BlackBerry would have led the touch-screen revolution in smartphones. For downstream players, technological shifts provide an opportunity to move customers to new criteria of purchase—to establish pole positions on these criteria. As a result of their focus on customer needs, the planning horizons of downstream-focused firms are practically infinite: as long as the customer segment exists, the firm will serve it.

The product range of a downstream-focused company is wider for two reasons. First, the downstream company attempts to offer complete solutions rather than stand-alone products to reduce the customers' costs and risks of purchase, consumption, disposal, and renewal. Often, this means both offering at least the option to purchase complementary products and offering services that will help reduce the costs and risks of purchase and use (e.g., search and consideration, purchase and installation, delivery, learning and training, service, maintenance, and disposal). The second reason that downstream-focused offerings have a broader range is that the firms ask what else the customer needs. They are trying to amortize the fixed costs of building trust and a favored relationship with the customer: they seek economies of scope as much as upstream players are obsessed with economies of scale.

Downstream-focused businesses tend to be multipronged. They have more points of contact with the customer throughout the organization.

Customer contact is no longer the monopoly of marketing and sales departments. In a business-to-business setting, the accounting department can learn about an international customer's need to receive invoices in a format that matches some particular cost-accounting needs. A minor change in the way invoices are presented saves the customer hours of data reentry. The logistics and shipping department engages with the receiving department at the customer end to integrate product flow. The purchasing department finds packaging that fits the stacking requirements in the customer's warehouse, reducing the customer's breakage and inventory-holding costs. Customers' costs and risks are reduced through each of these multiple points of contact.

Yet traditional firms, and in particular their marketing and sales departments, are often reluctant to allow too many points of contact. The reasons are obvious: they are trying to avoid the chaos of conflicting promises being made to the customer, and they want to make sure the customer gets a consistent and coherent message. That is an admirable reason to channel communications through a single point of contact, provided that the single point can indeed quarterback the entire relationship. In other words, can this point of contact identify opportunities to reduce costs and risks across the entire spectrum of activities and drive the various departments within the selling organization to deliver solutions that match customer needs? If marketing and sales departments take on this responsibility, they need to do much more than meet sales quotas and build and track brand performance. They need to take charge of the entire customer relationship, which includes the development of enduring solutions that reduce the customers' costs and risks of interacting with the firm.

Tilt and the Marketing and Sales Functions

You'd think that the marketing and sales functions would be the primary beneficiaries of a downstream tilt. As the center of gravity moves closer to the marketplace and to the customer, the activities that take place there become key to building lasting competitive advantage. Yet marketing, as a discipline, has been in a funk since the demise of mass marketing clipped its ability to move large numbers of customers to buy. Marketing has increasingly become tactical, moving the needle on share points, only to lose them within the quarter. In some companies, marketing is now relegated to issuing press releases and writing copy for external communications. No wonder marketers aren't making it to the top of organizations as they used to—what they're offering the business is no longer strategic. The data revolution was supposed to provide marketing with a renewed sense of purpose. Instead, it is either turning marketers into technicians trained on the next transaction or handing over customer management to technicians who understand data but not strategy.

This book offers marketing a means of contributing once again to building the firm's lasting competitive advantage. The perennial question that marketers must ask as a gateway into the strategic conversation is, "Why do our customers buy from us rather than from our competitors?" This question fulfills three objectives. First, it helps to uncover a firm's advantages over competitors in the eyes of the customer: which costs and risks the firm reduces better than its customers do, and which costs and risks are important to the customers. Second, the question identifies segments of customers that have a similar answer to the question. By grouping customers with similar answers, a firm can better target its offerings to different value segments. Finally, the question helps identify the criteria of purchase that a firm uses to position itself, differentiate itself from competitors, and capture valuable mind space.

In a downstream-focused organization, the marketing function takes on the task of identifying opportunities for downstream innovation. The examples in this book come from a wide variety of industries and show that the downstream innovations always developed systems that reduced customers' costs and risks. Whether the innovation occurs with a macro view of the marketplace or a micro view of the customer's mind, the system is developed centrally, not at the front line or in the field. Marketing must take charge of innovation and design a systematic (not ad hoc) solution to persistent problems that affect a large number of customers (not individual customers). A company's marketing department cannot expect to solve cost and risk problems for customers by simply adding head count to the sales force or otherwise empowering it or increasing service levels. However, customer satisfaction with the sales force will increase with the deployment of systematic solutions such as the never-empty silos deployed by MasterBuilders, the knowledge-based advice delivered by the agricultural inputs seller, the blast guarantees offered by ICI, or the lowering of the knowledge hurdle in the purchase of computers offered by Intel. In all cases, the sales force is also happier because the team has a differentiated offering that resonates with real customer needs.

A key strategic contribution of marketing continues to come from the management of the brand. But the tilt strategy suggests that the brand mainly competes in the customers' mind. The physical and digital worlds are merely the means for getting into this mind. Inside, the layout of the playing field (the outside boundaries defined by cognitive economy, the inside lines defined by criteria of purchase) and the rules of the game (consideration set formation, cutoff criteria versus trade-off criteria, exchange rates of trade-offs) are crucial to developing competitive advantage. This advantage is sustained through cognitive processes, for example, confirmatory biases when the customer is exposed to marketing information or product experience, as well as mechanisms like the endowment effect, customers' aversion to loss, and their purchase and consumption habits. The marketer who understands the value of these mechanisms plays a better competitive game.

Stepping back from how marketing functions in organizations to how it functions in the wider world is also revealing. Giant corporations that have mushroomed over the past decade have marketing at their core: Google, Amazon.com, Apple, and Facebook are all powered by marketing. Google and Facebook are media companies whose primary revenue comes from assembling and selling advertising access to customers; Apple extracts rent from its brand- and platform-building activities; and Amazon is a retailer. The value these companies create and capture, as well as their key competitive advantages, resides firmly downstream. The marketing function has never looked healthier.

The Global Competitive Landscape

Over the past three decades, the globalization of production and markets and the accompanying ballooning of global trade have changed the nature of markets and led to a geographic specialization that parallels the upstream-versus-downstream dichotomy. Players in developed markets have benefited from outsourcing production to contract manufacturers in China and other low-cost production centers. Firms in developed markets have both lowered their costs of procuring a finished product and turned previously fixed costs into variable ones—strategies that free up the time and resources to focus on higher-margin activities in acquiring, satisfying, and retaining customers. Simultaneously, producers in the production centers have benefited by gaining access to paying customers in the developed markets for the products spewing out of their ever-larger factories, but at lower margins.[2]

Despite the synergies of specialization, the business models of the two types of players could not be more different. In the markets of North America, Europe, and Japan, a pair of branded athletic shoes manufactured in China retails for between ten and twenty times its manufacturing cost. Similarly, for all the grief that Apple gets from many American commentators for not producing the iPhone in the United States, less than 10 percent of the iPhone's retail price is accounted for by production and sourcing activities in China, and less than 1 percent of its retail price is accounted for by labor costs in China. The remainder of the cost is mostly accounted for by activities such as R&D, design, management, branding, and retail sales—all activities that occur in the United States or other developed markets, in close proximity to customers. In contrast, the business model of manufacturers in Asia focuses on efficiency of production and thin margins on large volumes.

But the neat geographic separation of upstream and downstream activities is about to be challenged for two reasons. First, if there is one thing that manufacturers in Asia crave more than efficiency in delivering on their contracted manufacturing commitments, it is the long-term objective of moving up the value curve. Attracted by the hefty margins that manufacturers in Asia see their contract customers making on the products they've toiled over, the Asians are willing to learn new skills and take on more of the business activities that deliver those high returns. The phrase *moving up the value curve* is often thought to mean taking on functions such as design, new-product development, and even basic R&D to add value to and differentiate the products being manufactured. But many manufacturers are more ambitious. They interpret moving up the value curve to mean building a brand and a downstream infrastructure to serve end customers. So far, despite significant cost advantages in manufacturing, few emerging-market players have successfully built global brands that give them access to developed-market customers.[3] Lenovo, the Chinese computer manufacturer that purchased IBM's PC division; the household white-goods brand Haier; and the telecom equipment giant Huawei remain exceptions for now. The rarity of emerging-market global brands speaks to the difficulty of building downstream competitive advantage for players unaccustomed to playing there, as well as to the sustainability of the downstream advantages of existing players in the developed markets. But as more companies from emerging markets harbor ambitions of tilting than ever before, they will attempt to break down the downstream barriers, and the downstream will become the central battlefield for global competition.[4]

The second reason the geographic specialization of upstream and downstream is about to be challenged is the rapidly growing domestic consumption in emerging markets. Consumers in China still only consume less than one-tenth of what their American counterparts consume, and those in India consume less than one-twenty-fifth. But the middle class in both countries, as well as in many other large-population emerging markets such as Brazil, Mexico, Indonesia, Vietnam, Turkey, and South Africa, is rapidly joining the ranks of global consumers. Many multinationals expect more than half their revenue growth to come from these markets over the next ten years. The companies are investing in a downstream infrastructure, including brands and data, to serve these emerging customers. As they do, local firms in these emerging markets are also rapidly developing an appreciation for the importance of downstream activities—both as a competitive tool and as a source of lasting competitive advantage. That appreciation and the growth in downstream activities by emerging-market companies will further blur the geographic specialization of upstream and downstream activities—a separation that has characterized the global competitive landscape over the last thirty years. With this change, the downstream will become the primary competitive battleground in emerging markets.

For all firms around the world, the implications are clear. The downstream is the competitive playing field to watch. Your competitive advantage needs to be built and sustained in the marketplace, in your interactions with customers. The starting point for winning on this new playing field is to ask, why do your customers buy from you?

Notes

Chapter 1

1. Niraj Dawar and Jordan Mitchell, "Nestlé's Nescafé Partner's Blend: The Fairtrade Decision," Case 9B06A020 (Boston: Harvard Business School, 2006).

2. Morgen Witzel, *Fifty Key Figures in Management* (London: Routledge, 2003), 9–16.

3. Eric Bond et al., "Innovations of the Industrial Revolution: Agricultural Revolution," The Industrial Revolution web page, last updated February 17, 2003, http://industrialrevolution.sea.ca/innovations.html.

4. The section on Arkwright has benefited from discussions with John Bradley and is based on a similar section Bradley and I wrote jointly in "A Future History of Marketing," unpublished manuscript.

5. Kamran Kashani, "Innovation and Renovation: The Nespresso Story," Case IMD046 (Boston: Harvard Business School, 2000).

6. Liz Alderman, "Nespresso and Rivals View for Dominance in Coffee War," *New York Times,* August 20, 2010, www.nytimes.com/2010/08/21/business/global/21coffee.html?ref=coffee.

7. Philippe Silberzahn and Walter Van Dyck, *The Balancing Act of Innovation* (Leuven, Belgium: Lannoo, 2010).

8. Bryan Gruley and Cliff Edwards, "What Is Sony Now?" *Bloomberg BusinessWeek,* November 17, 2011, www.businessweek.com/printer/magazine/what-is-sony-now-11172011.html.

9. David Kravets, "RIIA Jury Finds Minnesota Woman Liable for Piracy, Awards $222,000," *Wired,* October 3, 2007, www.wired.com/threatlevel/2007/10/riaa-jury-finds/.

Chapter 2

1. Nick Bukley, "Hyundai's Guarantee Proves Attractive," *New York Times,* February 5, 2009, www.nytimes.com/2009/02/05/business/worldbusiness/05iht-auto.1.19948557.html.

2. I use the term *product* as a general term for an offering, which may be a product, a service, or a combination thereof.

3. IRI New Product Pacesetters report, April 2013, www.iriworldwide.com.

Chapter 3

1. Matt Lynley, "20 Reasons You Wish You Worked at a Tech Company: Free Laundry and Dry Cleaning!" *Business Insider,* July 30, 2012, www.businessinsider.com/the-best-perks-in-tech-2012-7#free-laundry-and-dry-cleaning-5.

2. Thomas N. Robinson, Dina L. G. Borzekowski, Donna M. Matheson, and Helena C. Kraemer, "Effects of Fast Food Branding on Young Children's Taste Preferences," *Archives of Pediatric and Adolescent Medicine* 161, no. 8 (2007): 792–797.

Chapter 4

1. R. Collins and M. Gibbs, "ICI: Nobel's Explosives Company," Case IMD-6-0170 (Boston: Harvard Business School, 1995); R. Schmenner, "ICI: Nobel's explosives company, Abridged" Case IMD-6-0241 (2002), IMD Lausanne, Switzerland; Mark Vandenbosch and Niraj Dawar, "Beyond Better Products: Capturing Value in Customer Interactions," *MIT Sloan Management Review* 43, no. 4 (2002): 35–42.

2. Vandenbosch and Dawar, "Beyond Better Products."

3. Michael Korda, *Making the List: A Cultural History of the American Bestseller, 1900–1999* (New York: Barnes and Noble Books–Imports, 2001).

4 Sabine Begall et al., "Magnetic Alignment in Grazing and Resting Cattle and Deer," *Proceedings of the National Academy of Sciences* 105, no. 36 (September 9, 2008): 13,451–13,455.

5. Hyneck Burda et al., "Extremely Low-Frequency Electromagnetic Fields Disrupt Magnetic Alignment of Ruminants," *Proceedings of the National Academy of Sciences* 106, no. 14 (April 7, 2009): 5,708–5,713.

6. Mark Twain, *Tom Sawyer and Huckleberry Finn,* 2nd ed. (Hertfordshire, UK: Wordsworth Editions, 1992), 214.

7. Johan Bolen, Huina Mao, and Xiaojun Zeng, "Twitter Mood Predicts the Stock Market," *Journal of Computational Science* 2, no. 1 (2011): 1–8.

8. Scott A. Golder and Michael W. Macy, "Diurnal and Seasonal Mood Vary with Work, Sleep, and Daylength Across Diverse Cultures," *Science* 333 (2011): 1,878–1,881.

9. See www.businessinsider.com/twitter-bluefin-labs-2013-2.

Chapter 5

1. "Nina™ Is the First Virtual Assistant to Understand What Is Said—And Who Is Saying It; First to Provide an Open SDK for Mobile App Developers," Nuance website, August 6, 2012, www.nuance.com/company/news-room/press-releases/Nuance-Introduces-Nina.docx.

2. Thomas D. Jensen, "Comparison Processes in Energy Conservation Feedback Effects," *Advances in Consumer Research* 13 (1986): 486–491. See also John E. Petersen et al., "Dormitory Residents Reduce Electricity Consumption When Exposed to Real-Time Visual Feedback and Incentives," *International Journal of Sustainability in Higher Education* 8, no. 1 (2007): 16–33; L. J. Becker, "Joint Effect of Feedback and Goal Setting on Performance: A Field Study of Residential Energy Conservation," *Journal of Applied Psychology* 63 (1978): 428–433; and L. J. Becker, C. Seligman, and J. Darley, "Psychological Strategies to Reduce Energy Consumption: Project Summary Report," Report PU/CEES 90 (Princeton, NJ: Center for Energy and Environmental Studies, Princeton University, 1979).

3. Don Peppers, "Social Media's Envy Effect," *Fast Company,* December 21, 2011, www.fastcompany.com/1803069/social-medias-envy-effect. See also Michael J. Coren, "Plugging Your Utility Bill into Facebook to Compete with Friends," accessed April 18, 2013, www.fastcoexist.com/1678956/plugging-your-utility-bill-into-facebook-to-compete-with-friends.

4. Anthony G. Hopwood, "The Rankings Game: Reflections on Devinney, Dowling and Perm-Ajchariyawong," *European Management Review* 5 (2008): 209–214.

5. Ian Gordon, "Measuring Customer Relationships: What Gets Measured Really Does Get Managed," Reprint 9B03TD02, *Ivey Business Journal Online,* July–August 2003.

Chapter 6

1. Mark Pendergrast, *For God, Country, and Coca-Cola: The Definitive History of the Great American Soft Drink and the Company That Makes It,* 3rd ed. (New York: Basic Books, 2013).

2. For Interbrand rankings, see "Best Global Brands 2012," Interbrand web page, accessed May 18, 2013, http://www.interbrand.com/en/best-global-brands/2012/Best-Global-Brands-2012-Brand-View.aspx.

3. Eleanor Rosch, "Principles of Categorization," in *Cognition and Categorization,* ed. Eleanor Rosch and Barbara B. Lloyd (Hillsdale, NJ: Lawrence Erlbaum, 1978), 27–48.

4. Jacob Goldenberg, Donald R. Lehmann, and David Mazursky, "The Idea Itself and the Circumstances of Its Emergence as Predictors of New Product Success," *Management Science* 47, no. 1 (2001): 69–84, and IRI New Product Pacesetters report, April 2013, www.iriworldwide.com.

5. Mary Tripsas, "It's Brand New, but Make It Sound Familiar," *New York Times,* October 4, 2009, Business section.

Chapter 7

1. Gerard J. Tellis and Peter N. Golder, "First to Market, First to Fail? Real Causes of Enduring Market Leadership," *MIT Sloan Management Review,* winter 1996, 65–75. See also Gerard J. Tellis and Peter N. Golder, "Pioneer Advantage: Market Logic or Market Legend?" *Journal of Marketing Research* 30 (May 1993): 158–170.

2. Of course, you can Google it. The web remembers it, so you don't have to. But consider that the second person to cross the Atlantic solo was also a first in another category: she was the first woman to cross the Atlantic, solo. And because she was first, you now remember her name: Amelia Earhart.

3. Gregory S. Carpenter and Kent Nakamoto, "Consumer Preference Formation and Pioneering Advantage," *Journal of Marketing Research* 28, no. 3 (1989): 285–298.

4. Ibid., 286.

5. Mark Parry, "Cialis," Case UV2938 (Charlottesville: University of Virginia Darden Graduate School of Business Administration, 2003).

6. Elie Ofek, "Product Team Cialis: Getting Ready to Market," Case 505038 (Boston: Harvard Business School, 2004).

7. Parry, "Cialis," 9.

8. Ibid., 6.

9. Michael Arndt, "Is Viagra Vulnerable?," *BusinessWeek,* October 27, 2003, 70.

10. Duff Wilson, "As Generics Near, Makers Tweak Erectile Drugs," *New York Times,* April 13, 2011, www.nytimes.com/2011/04/14/health/14pills.html.

11. "Usage Guidelines for the Intel Insider® Trademark," Intel web page, accessed April 19, 2013, www.intel.com/pressroom/intel_inside.htm.

12. Gordon E. Moore, "Cramming More Components onto Integrated Circuits," *Electronics Magazine* 38, no. 8 (April 1965): 4.

13. Wikipedia, s.v. "Moore's Law," last updated April 3, 2013, http://en.wikipedia.org/wiki/Moore's_law.

14. David Weinstein, "Intel Inside," Case 594-038-1 (Fontainebleau: INSEAD, 1994).

15. Ibid., 1.

16. Ibid.

17. "iPhones Make Chinese Eyes Light Up," *Economist,* July 28, 2012, www.economist.com/node/21559624.

18. The shampoo example comes from Gregory S. Carpenter, Rashi Glazer, and Kent Nakamoto, "Meaningful Brands from Meaningless Differentiation: The

Dependence on Irrelevant Attributes," *Journal of Marketing Research* 31 (August 1994): 339–350.

19. David Pogue, "Spec Obsession Disorder: The Incurable Techie Malady," *New York Times,* April 5, 2012, http://pogue.blogs.nytimes.com/2012/04/05/spec-obsession-disorder-the-incurable-techie-malady/.

20. "The Oreo Case," Ban Trans Fats website, accessed April 19, 2013, www.bantransfats.com/theoreocase.html.

21. Sebastian Anthony, "The History of Kodak: Pioneer of Film and Digital Photography," *Extreme Tech,* October 12, 2011, http://tinyurl.com/bv4dvc9.

22. Kevin Roose, "New RIM Chief Not Looking to Split Company," *Dealbook* (financial news service of the New York Times), January 23, 2012, http://dealbook.nytimes.com/2012/01/23/new-rim-chief-not-looking-to-split-company/.

Chapter 8

1. James R. Bettman, Mary Frances Luce, and John W. Payne, "Constructive Consumer Choice Processes," *Journal of Consumer Research* 25 (1998): 187–217.

2. Joseph W. Alba and Amitava Chattopadhyay, "Salience Effects in Brand Recall," *Journal of Marketing Research* 23 (1986): 363–369; Joseph W. Alba and Amitava Chattopadhyay, "Brand Evaluations," *Journal of Consumer Research* 17 (December 1986): 263–276. See also Raymond S. Nickerson, "Retrieval Inhibition from Part-Set Cuing: A Persisting Enigma in Memory Research," *Memory and Cognition* 12, no. 6 (1984): 531–552.

3. Robert F. Bornstein, "Exposure and Affect: Overview and Meta-Analysis of Research," *Psychological Bulletin* 106, no. 2 (1989): 265–289.

Chapter 9

1. Eric Jackson, "How Jim Balsillie First Discussed the Competitive Threat of iPhone to the BlackBerry," *Forbes,* September 16, 2011, http://tinyurl.com/43713f6.

2. See http://bgr.com/2013/04/02/iphone-5s-release-date-china-mobile-410928/.

3. See http://www.engadget.com/2012/12/06/idc-apple-slipped-to-sixth-in-china-smartphone-share-during-q3/.

4. Niraj Dawar, "Expect the Unexpected," *Just Marketing,* May 22, 2011, http://nothingbutmarketing.blogspot.ca/2011/05/expect-unexpected.html.

Chapter 10

1. Pierre Chandon, J. Wesley Hutchinson, Eric T. Bradlow, and Scott H. Young, "Does In-Store Marketing Work? Effects of the Number and Position

of Shelf Facings on Brand Attention and Evaluation at the Point of Purchase," *Journal of Marketing* 73, no. 6 (2009): 1–17.

2. John Deighton, "The Interaction of Advertising and Evidence," *Journal of Consumer Research* 11 (December 1984): 763–770; Stephen J. Hoch and Young-Won Ha, "Consumer Learning: Advertising and the Ambiguity of Product Experience," *Journal of Consumer Research* 13 (September 1986): 221–233; Nitin Mehta, Xinlei (Jack) Chen, and Om Narasimhan, "Informing, Transforming, and Persuading: Disentangling the Multiple Effects of Advertising on Brand Choice Decisions," *Marketing Science* 27, no. 3 (2008): 334–355.

3. Niraj Dawar, "In Brands We Trust: Why Do Consumers Trust Brands?" *Just Marketing*, June 19, 2011, http://nothingbutmarketing.blogspot.ca/2011/06/in-brands-we-trust.html.

4. Hugo Mercier and Dan Sperber, "Why Do Humans Reason? Arguments for an Argumentative Theory," *Behavioral and Brain Sciences* 34 (2011): 57–111.

5. Nathan Novemsky and Daniel Kahneman, "The Boundaries of Loss Aversion," *Journal of Marketing Research* 42 (2005): 119–128; Dan Ariely, Joel Huber, and Klaus Wertenbroch, "When Do Losses Loom Larger Than Gains?" *Journal of Marketing Research* 42 (2005): 134–138; Michal A. Strahilevitz and George F. Lowenstein, "The Effect of Ownership History on the Valuation of Objects," *Journal of Consumer Research* 25 (December 1998): 276–289.

Chapter 11

1. Laurence Capron and Will Mitchell, *Build, Borrow, or Buy?* (Boston: Harvard Business Review Press, 2012).

2. Joe Weisenthal, "The Great Migration: How Asian and Western Companies Completely Switched Roles in 15 Years," *Business Insider,* March 15, 2012, www.businessinsider.com/sales-go-east-margins-go-west-2012-3.

3. Niraj Dawar and Tony Frost, "Competing with Giants: Survival Strategies for Local Companies in Emerging Markets," *Harvard Business Review,* March–April 1999.

4. Amitava Chattopadhyay, Rajeev Batra, and Asequl Ozsomer, *The New Emerging Market Multinationals: Four Big Strategies for Disrupting Markets and Building Brands* (New York: McGraw Hill, 2012).

Index

About the Author

NIRAJ DAWAR, Professor at the Ivey Business School (Canada and Hong Kong), is a renowned marketing strategy expert who has also served on the faculty of leading business schools in Europe and Asia. He works with senior leadership in global companies and has executed assignments for BMW, HSBC, Microsoft, Cadbury, L'Oréal, and McCain Foods on three continents. He has also worked with start-ups in the biotech and information space. His publications have appeared in *Harvard Business Review*, *MIT Sloan Management Review*, and in leading academic journals. His press commentary has appeared in the *Financial Times*, the *International Herald Tribune*, and the *Globe and Mail*. He lives in Canada.